CONSUMER PROTECTION IN HOSPITALITY, TRAVEL AND TOURISM

CONSUMER PROTECTION IN HOSPITALITY, TRAVEL AND TOURISM

GULSHAN SONI

Ph.D. in Hotel Management and Tourism (U.S.A.)
M.Phil. Tourism Management, MSc HM & CT,
Executive MBA, Diploma in Training & Development,
G.H.O.T.P. (Jaypee Hotels Limited)

AMAN PUBLICATIONS

NEW DELHI

Published by
Rajiv Jain for Aman Publications
LG-4A, Ganpati Bhawan,
4675-B/21, Ansari Road,
Darya Ganj, Delhi - 110002
PH: 23255012, 23282127
E-mail: sshjbs@yahoo.com

First Published – 2011

ISBN–81–8204–058-2
97881-8204-058-2

SOLE DISTRIBUTOR
JINDAL BOOK SERVICES
LG-4A, Ganpati Bhawan,
4675-B/21, Ansari Road,
Darya Ganj, Delhi - 110002

Printed by:
Sachin Printers, Delhi.

Preface

The present work is an effort to throw light on "CONSUMER PROTECTION IN HOSPITALITY, TRAVEL AND TOURISM" The work would not have been possible to come to the present shape without the able guidance of number of people and it has become possible because of their appreciable support.

Hospitality industry is the most diverse and specialized industry in the world. The emerging role of private sector in planning, organizing, managing and financing in the hospitality industry and the introduction of hospitality courses at senior secondary level by some of state boards shows the importance of hospitality in the diverse and the dynamic modern era.

Their insights and inputs have immensely helped me in understanding the core issues of consumer protection in the hospitality industry. This research is an attempt of marking a beginning towards the detailed analysis of consumer protection and its subsequent relation to the Travel & Tourism Industry.

I am sure that this book will prove to be a source of inspiration and enlightens of knowledge each page will awaken a longing to pick up the phone and talk to me.

I express my gratitude to the management of Banarasidas Chandi Wala Institute of Hotel Management and Caterering Technology, and Shri. Bhuwan Mohan ji, Secretary, Shri Banarsidas Chandiwala Sewa Smarak Trust Society for their motivation and encouragement to undertake this relatively less explored but highly poignant area of hospitality. I also extend my thanks to Principal Mr. R.K. Bhandri and Deputy Director Administration Mr. Pradeep Gupta, for their altruistic support.

I would like to thanks Mr. Rajeev Jain and Mr. Sanjeev Jain of M/s Aman Publications for their persistence and support. Finally I would to thanks to all my friends and my well wishers.

GULSHAN SONI

Contents

1

INTRODUCTION

INDIAN TRAVEL AND TOURISM INDUSTRY- AN OVERVIEW

The conventional 'construct' of travel and tourism industry in any economy is based on the notion of tourists visiting places of historical and religious importance. There are three problems with such an approach.

- There is an implicit notion that, so far as, heritage is a preserve of the country, and tourism is primarily a concern of the State.
- The construct does not include other aspects, and hence, is restrictive. It does not reflect the pluralism about the tourism.
- It tends to ignore the new thrust created by globalization that permits an enormous potential for an economic advantage through tourism and travel, on an individual basis, for each country, and collectively for the whole world. Tourism industry is one of the largest employers in world. These limitations point out towards the need for a paradigm shift. Travel and tourism need not

> be primarily a concern of the State. The 'construct' of tourism is a 'complex whole'. It is by nature pluralistic. And above all, unless travel and tourism is understood, and treated, as an industry, it cannot be self-sustaining.

With more disposable income and interest in traveling for leisure and business, the travel and tourism industries are big businesses in the global as well as at the domestic level and have become influential forces in the economy. Tourism is concerned with encouraging, entertaining and assisting business travelers and tourists, while the travel industry covers tour operators and travel agents who arrange and coordinate travel within the country and abroad. Travel industry includes airlines, cruise ships, luxury bus services, and railways, to name a few that transport people to their chosen destination. The tourist inflow into the country touched a new high of 34.5 lakh in June 2008 and tourism experts are hopeful that the trend is going to continue in coming 2008-09 as well. The forex from tourism registered a 23 per cent increase and touched Rs 21,828 crore. India got Gold awards in Pacific Asia Travel Association (PATA) meet, including two for the state of Kerala and two for the Ministry of Tourism. Some people in tourism and travel management work behind the scenes, while others meet people all the time. There are jobs for those who enjoy planning ahead and making money and others for people whose interest is in helping the public as best as they can. At the Central and the state government levels, officers in the administrative services are posted to the tourism department. In the private sector, travel management professionals find placement in tour companies, travel agencies, among others. According to estimates, one out of every nine jobs in the world will be generated by the travel and tourism industry. A career in the travel industry opens up a world of opportunities ensuring growth opportunities and excellent pay packets.

Tourism is one of the fastest growing industries in the world today. Tourism is presently India's second largest net foreign exchange earning exporting industry after textile or garment. The tourism industry in India is witnessing a whopping 30% Yearly growth. The foreign exchange revenue stands at about 21,828 Crore which has been highest for last 10 years. India's travel industry is thriving due to an increase in foreign tourist visiting India as well as the rise in domestic tourist. Visitors are pouring in from all parts of the world: specially from Europe. The trend has changed a lot as compared to few years back. Even in summers tourist are coming out to experience the beauty of resorts in Himalayan Mountains range. The growth of the tourism sector of Indian economy at present huge. This has become one of the major industrial sectors in the Indian Economy .The tourism industry earns the foreign exchange of worth Rs 21,828 crore annually. In the 2008 the growth rate of tourism sector of Indian Economy was recorded 17.3%.The growth of tourism industry is due to the rise in the arrival of more and more foreign tourists and the increase in the number of domestic tourists . The recent terror attacks on Mumbai 26/11, 11 September 2001 Bali Bombing, Marriott Hotel in Islamabad and the 9/11 has created a concern over the tourist traveling more, however that has been worked as a catalyst for Indian tourism industry. With SARS, Tsunami, Kashmir issues and more recently is Financial turmoil, it was believed that the negative trend in on the doorstep however such kind is seen in last couple of months. In last few months the global aviation tourists loses $5billion and in hotels there was already 30% cut in room rates after recent Mumbai attack. Hoteliers and Industry expects a sharp rise in domestic tourism in coming months almost 95% on travel and tourism market dependent on domestic travelers .There are several reasons for the boom, however categorically there may be 4 reasons.

1. Online access of booking.
2. Cut down in room rates and tour packages
3. Indian Government Initiative:-

Recently the ministry has announced of investing more in the industry. In the recent budget, Finance Minister P.Chidambaram announced a good amount of money to be invested in travel industry. Aggressive advertising campaign "Incredible India" by the government has also had contribution in changing India's image a lot.

4. Global tourism has dropped:-

Globally the tourism industry has seen a down turn. This has helped India a lot. More foreign tourist are now focusing on India as well as south Asian countries.

5. More aviation options to India:-

Recently there was almost a flow of announces of new flights to and from India. This has helped the tourist having more option suiting to their timings. There is no doubt there will be better facilities in India would be available very soon. Ultimately more people will travel across the country to explore the hidden beauties that has been uncovered for years. All these factors have also contributed to the overall travel and tourism industry of one of the major heartlands of the country; New Delhi.

The estimated foreign exchange earning during January to December 08 were $ 4916.01 million as compared to $ 4819.62 million during the same periods of 2007, showing an increase of 3.4 %. Foreign tourist's arrival has gone up to 575148 during 2007 registering a growth of 4.8% as compared to 2006. Tourism is not only a major social phenomenon of the modern society like that of New Delhi but with enormous economic consequences but also the world largest export industry which accounts for about 8 %of the total world's export more than 30% of International trade in services, 10.7%

of the global work force and about 12 % of the world GDP. It is also dubbed as the largest smokeless industry and contributes towards preservations of clean environment The year 2005-06 saw tourism emerging as one of the major sectors for growth of Indian economy, the foreign exchange earnings increased from Rs. 16,429 crore to 21,828 crore up to December. Tourism also contributed to the economy indirectly through its linkages with other sectors like horticulture, agriculture, poultry, handicrafts and construction. Similarly in the last year, tourism industry registered a growth rate of 17.3% in foreign tourist arrivals, which has been the highest in last 10 years. Foreign exchange earnings grew at an even higher rate 30.2%. The pattern and trend of travel and tourism industry in New Delhi is a reflection of the broader scope of the same industry in the country with certain minor deviations so far as the southern travel and tourism industry is concerned.

Foreign Tourist Arrivals (FTAs)

- FTAs during the year 2008 were 5.37 million as compared to FTAs of 5.08 million during the year 2007. Therefore, in spite of global financial meltdown and terrorist activities, numbers of FTAs have increased in 2008 as compared to 2007. UNWTO has predicted a growth rate of 2-3% for international tourist arrivals in the world during 2008. Therefore, Indian Scenario (growth rate of 5.6%) is much better than world scenario.
- The number of FTAs in December 2008 has risen to 5.22 lakhs as compared to 5.21 lakhs in November 2008.
- Foreign Exchange Earnings (FEE) from Tourism in Indian rupee terms and US' $ terms .FEE during the year 2008 were Rs. 50730 crore as compared to Rs. 44360 crore in 2007.

- FEE in US $ terms during for the year 2008 were US $ 11747 million as compared to FEE of US $ 10729 during 2007. The lower growth rate in 2008 as compared to 2007 may be mainly due to lower growth rate of FTAs in 2008 as compared to 2007 and exchange rate variation.
- FEE from tourism in December 2008 were Rs. 5083 crore as compared to Rs. 4935 crore in November 2008 and Rs. 5079 crore in December 2007.
- FEE in US $ terms during the year 2008 were US $ 1046 million as compared to US $ 1005 million in November 2008 and US $ 1287 million in December 2007. The decline in the FEE in US $ term during December 2008 vis-à-vis December 2007 is mainly due to the foreign exchange variations in these months.

Outbound Tourism Statistics

Destination Wise Outbound Travel of Indian Nationals

	2000	2001	2002	2003	2004	2005
Canada	52071	54742	55492	57010	68315	77849
USA	274202	26967	257271	272161	308845	344926
Bangladesh	74268	78090	80415	84704	80469	86231
Maldives	10616	8511	11377	11502	10999	10260
Nepal	96995	63722	65743	86578	89861	95685
Pakistan	66061	58378	2618	7096	19658	59560
Sri Lanka	31860	33924	69960	90603	105151	113323
Malaysia	132127	143513	183360	145153	172966	225789
Singapore	346356	339813	375658	309446	471196	583543
Thailand	224104	206132	253110	230316	300163	352766
China	120930	159361	213611	219097	309411	356460
Australia	41452	48227	45022	45597	55603	67951
Hong Kong	131368	161752	193705	178130	244364	273487
Japan	38767	40345	45394	47520	53000	58572

Source: Ministry of Tourism.

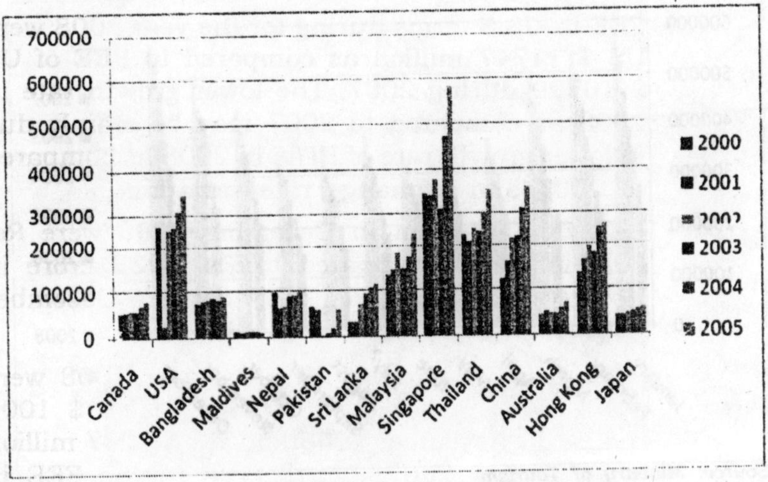

Source: Ministry of Tourism

Inbound Tourism Statistics

Foreign Tourists In India (Number)

	2001	2002	2003	2004	2005	2006	2007	2008
January	283750	228150	274215	337345	385977	459489	532088	584765
February	262306	227529	262692	331697	369844	439090	498806	560658
March	248965	225558	218473	293185	352094	391009	444186	509926
April	185338	155378	160941	223884	248416	309208	333945	369677
May	151098	132998	141508	185502	225394	255008	267758	290785
June	176716	143100	176324	223122	246970	278370	310104	344526
July	224432	186432	225359	272456	307870	337332	377474	-
August	196517	161477	204940	253301	273856	304387	360089	-
September	162326	151721	191339	226773	257184	297891	325893	-
October	181605	212191	260569	307447	347757	391399	440715	-
November	209685	243566	290583	385238	423837	442413	510987	-
December	-	-	319271	417527	479411	541571	575148	-

Source: Ministry of Tourism

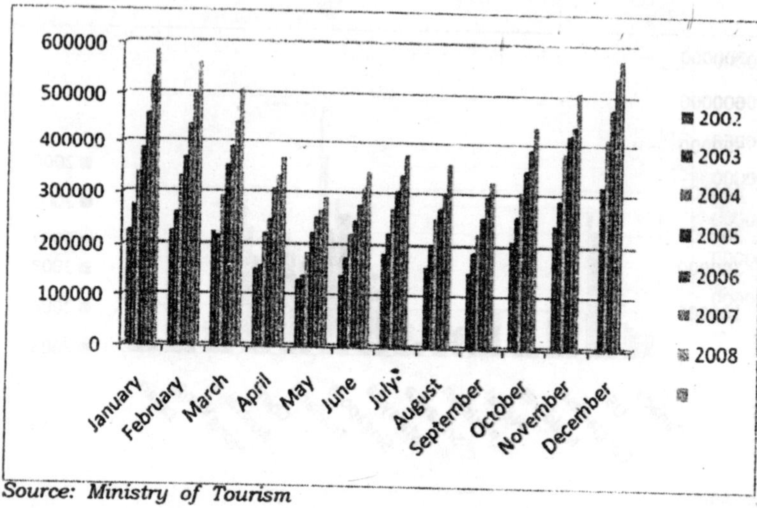

Source: Ministry of Tourism

International Tourists Arrivals to India

Arrivals from Region/ Country	2001	2002	2003	2004	2005	2006
USA	329147	348182	410803	526120	611165	696739
UK	405472	387846	430917	555907	651803	734240
Canada	88600	93598	107671	135884	157643	176567
Germany	80011	64891	76868	116679	120243	156808
France	102434	78194	97654	131824	152258	175345
Australia	52691	50743	58730	81608	96258	109867
Italy	41351	37136	46908	65561	67642	79978
Japan	80634	59709	77996	96851	103082	119292
Malaysia	57869	63748	70750	84390	96276	107286
Singapore	42824	44306	48368	60710	68666	82574
Nepal	41135	37136	42771	51534	77024	91552
Sri Lanka	112813	108008	109098	128711	136400	154813
Netherlans	42368	31669	40565	51211	52755	58611
China	13901	15422	21152	34100	44897	62330
South Korea	27150	29374	35584	47835	49895	705407

Source: Ministry of Tourism

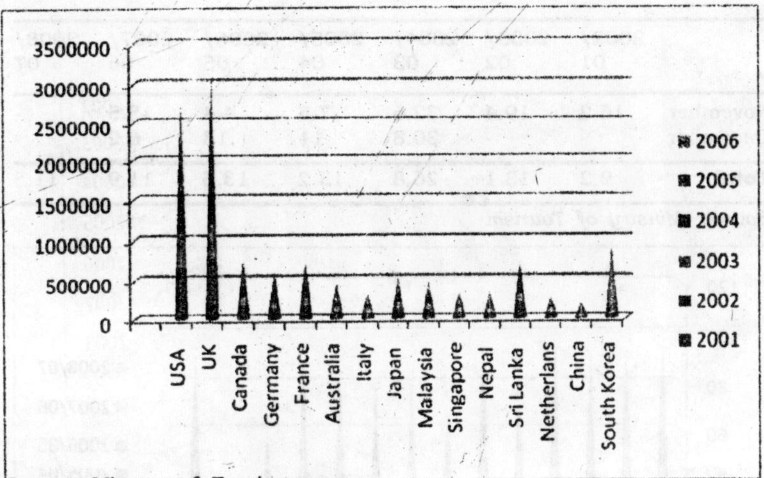

Source: Minstry of Tourism

Delhi tourism Statistics

Domestic Tourists Statistics - Delhi

Year	Domestic Tourists
2004	1866552
2005	2061782
2006	2237130

Source: Delhi Tourism

Percentage Changes in foreign tourists arrival

	2002/ 01	2003/ 02	2004/ 03	2005/ 04	2006/ 05	2007/ 06	2008/ 07
January	-19.6	22	23	14.5	19	15.8	9.9
February	-13.3	13.1	26.3	17.3	18.7	13.6	12.4
March	-9.4	1.6	34.2	25.2	11.1	13.6	14.8
April	-16.2	5	39.1	16.5	24.5	8	10.7
May	-12	0.2	31.1	23.8	13.1	5	8.6
June	-19	27.5	26.5	16	12.7	11.4	11.1
July	-16.9	22.5	20.9	7.3	9.6	11.9	-
August	-17.8	26.91	23.6	6.9	11.1	18.3	-
September	-6.5	26.11	18.5	11.4	15.8	9.4	-
October	16.8	22.11	18	7	12.5	12.6	-

	2002/ 01	2003/ 02	2004/ 03	2005/ 04	2006/ 05	2007/ 06	2008/ 07
November	16.2	19.4	32.6	7.8	4.4	15.5	-
December	-	-	30.8	11	13	6.2	-
Total	9.2	13.1	26.8	13.2	13.5	11.9	11.5

Source: Minstry of Tourism

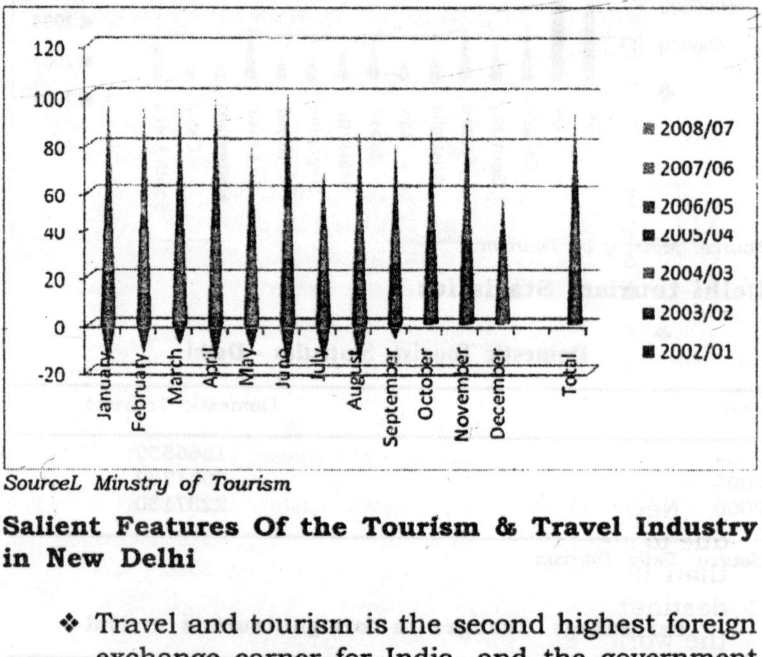

SourceL Minstry of Tourism

Salient Features Of the Tourism & Travel Industry in New Delhi

- Travel and tourism is the second highest foreign exchange earner for India, and the government has given organizations in this industry export house status. The industry is waking up to the potential of domestic tourism as well, with an estimated 4.7 billion domestic trips in 2001. Tourism spending within India in 2001 was US$ 22 billion. New Delhi, being the Capital of India with major historical places in and near it is a major tourist attraction.
- There is considerable government presence in the travel and tourism industry. Each state has a

tourism corporation, which typically runs a chain of hotels /motels and operates package tours, while the central government runs the India Tourism Development Corporation. Divestment of these state-run tourism corporations have either already taken place or are in process. The state government of Delhi has also its own tourism and travel promotion boards and places like Dilli Haat.

- Incoming foreign tourist arrivals have shown a 6% compounded annual growth rate over the last 10 years. The government has realized the potential and has advanced several incentives to promote infrastructure growth in the tourism sector. The tourist infrastructure growth in Delhi/ New Delhi is a clear indication of this.
- Current investments are likely to see hotel room capacity increase by 20% over the next three years, with several international hotel chains entering the hotel industry. Similar growth is anticipated in air travel capacity.

New Delhi's travel and tourism industry is thriving due to an increase in foreign tourists' arrivals and greater than before travel by Indians to domestic and abroad destinations. The visitors are pouring in from all over the world: Europe, Africa, Southeast Asia and Australia. At the same time, the number of Indians traveling has also increased. Some tourists come from Middle East countries to witness the drenching monsoon rains in India, a phenomenon never seen in desert climates. These tourists can resist the temptation to visit Delhi before leaving for their country. Domestic tourists are also fueling the industry's revival. Many of them escape from the summer heat on the plains to resorts in the Himalayan Mountains. One of the major beneficiaries this year is Kashmir, where a cease-fire between India and Pakistan has reduced violence, if not completely, at least enough to help revive the state's sagging tourism industry. Among the most favoured tourist destinations in India, Kerala for its scenic beauty, Agra for Taj Mahal, Khajarao for its sculptures and temples, Goa for its beaches and some pilgrimages are the most important. Delhi is a major tourist spot due to its historical importance.

Interesting feature of this growth is that it has come even as global tourism has dropped, due to the September 11 terrorist attacks in the United States, the outbreak of Severe Acute Respiratory Syndrome in East Asia, and the Iraq war. Even the disastrous tsunami didn't affect India's tourism industry, as tourist arrivals in India rose 23.5 percent in Dec 2004 and tourist arrivals crossed 3 million mark for the first time in 2004. The disaster was expected to have a negative impact on India's tourism in terms of large-scale cancellations of tourists to India but nothing of that sort was seen.

Contribution of Travel and Tourism to GDP and Employment

	World Average(%)	India (%)	World Rank
Contribution of Tourism and Travel Economy to GDP	10.7	5.3	140
Contribution of Tourism and Travel Industry to GDP	4.2	2.5	124
Contribution of Travel and Tourism Economy Employment	8	5.6	140
Contribution of Travel and Tourism Industry Employment	3.1	2.9	111

Source: WTTC, Department of Tourism, Government of India.

International Tourist Arrivals

	Million		Growth Rate (%)		Market Share (%)	
	1999	2000*	1999/ 1998	2000*/ 1999	1999	2000*
World	650.0	698.3	3.8	7.4	100	100
Africa	26.5	26.9	6.1	1.5	4.1	3.8
America	122.3	130.2	2.3	6.5	18.8	18.6
East Asia/Pacific	97.6	111.7	10.8	14.5	15.0	16.0
Europe	379.8	403.3	1.7	6.2	58.4	57.8
Middle East	18.1	20.0	18.1	10.2	2.8	2.9
South Asia	5.8	6.3	10.7	9.0	0.9	0.9

Source: World Tourism Organisation.
** As collected from WTO database in January 2001.*

The World Tourism Organization forecast indicates an increasing tourism preference towards East Asia, the Pacific, West Asia and South Asia, although Europe and America still remain the world's foremost tourism destinations commanding 77 per cent of the global market. East Asia/Pacific achieved the highest rate of growth of 14.5 per cent in tourism and travel in 2000 followed by West Asia and South Asia. With this gradual shift in focus, the outlook for the growth of tourism in the region is promising. In Asia, China has emerged as a leading tourist destination and is poised to become the world's top tourist destination by 2020. The WTTC has identified India as one of the world's foremost tourist growth centers in the coming decade. After Turkey, India is expected to achieve the fastest rate of growth of the total amount of economic activity likely to be generated by travel and tourism, at 9.7 per cent over the next 10 years. Also, the largest employment creation after China is expected to take place in India over the same period. The growth in 'visitor exports' or spending by international tourists, is likely to be the fastest in India at 14.3 per cent per annum over the next decade. On the whole, the WTTC forecast for India is promising, subject to key policy issues that affect the growth of the sector being addressed. New Delhi with its huge travel and tourism infrastructure can not be expected to lag behind to attract the tourists, both domestic and foreign.

Delhi receives the largest number of overseas tourists from the United Kingdom, which is its largest source market, followed by the United States, Sri Lanka, France, Germany, Canada, Japan, Australia and Singapore. Of the tourists coming to Delhi, 27.5 per cent are in the age group of 35-44 years, 23.4 per cent in the age group of 25-35 years and 20.8 per cent in the age group of 45-54 years. Women constitute only 30.5 per cent of India's total international arrivals. Repeat visitors account for 44.9 per cent of the overseas visitors. A substantial number of these may be non-resident Indians, as hotel reservations* do not correspond to the number of international arrivals in the country. The average length of stay of foreign tourists in the country in 1998 was 31.2 days. Domestic tourism, on the other hand, is largely pilgrimage-oriented and requires improvement in travel facilities and pilgrim destinations.

International and Domestic Tourism

	World	India	Percentage share of India
International Arrivals	698 million	2.64 million	0.38%
Tourism Receipts	$595 billion	$3.2 billion	0.69%
Domestic tourism Worldwide	6,980 million	210 million	4.6%

Delhi being an historic as well as the capital city receives a large number of tourists, from abroad and from other parts of the country.

Reasons for This Boom

There could be several reasons for the buoyancy in the Indian tourism industry and the simultaneous growth in the Capital of Delhi. First, the upward trend observed in the growth rate of Indian economy has raised middle class incomes, prompting more people to spend money on vacations abroad or at home. This is more evident in a developed metro like Delhi. Also, Delhi is booming in the information technology industry and has become the IT center with Gurgaon and Noida around it. Aggressive advertising campaign "Incredible India" by the government and Bhagidari by the Government of Delhi have also had contribution in changing Delhi's image from that of a land of deserts, and sparking new interest among overseas travelers.

Tourism Contribution to the Economy

It is not hidden that tourism is among India's important export industries and this theoretical assumption also holds good for the Delhi and NCR. Even with comparatively low levels of international tourist traffic, tourism has already emerged as an important segment of the state economy. Tourism also contributed to the economy indirectly through its linkages with other sectors like horticulture, agriculture, poultry, handicrafts and construction. Foreign exchange earnings from tourism during 2003-04 were US $ 3,533 million (Rs 16,429 crore). Besides being an important foreign exchange earner, tourism industry also provides employment to millions of people in India both directly and indirectly (through its linkage with other sectors of the economy.) It is estimated that total direct employment in the tourism sector is around 20 million.

Barriers to Growth

There are several factors that are responsible for the inadequate growth of the tourism sector in Delhi. These are: barriers related to approach, barriers that discourage private investment, factors that affect competitiveness and factors that affect the long-term sustainability of tourism. The effective and early removal of these barriers during the Tenth Plan is an essential determinant for the success of the New Tourism Policy. The need for a national consensus on the role and level of tourism development in the country has been voiced repeatedly but a concerted effort to achieve a consensus has not been made. Tourism should not be limited by state or regional boundaries if distortions in policies are to be avoided. It is important that a consensus among all states is evolved through the National Development Council (NDC) and the barriers to the growth of tourism removed.

Approach-Related Barriers

- Absence of consensus on role of tourism.
- Lack of priority to tourism on account of unappreciated potential.
- Relatively lowlevels of investment.
- Lack of interest on the part of the state government - the primary players.
- An unprofessional ad hoc approach.

Tourism has been denied the priority it deserves over successive Plan periods because its potential as an engine of economic growth has not been appreciated. This is visible in the low allocation of resources. Most State Governments gives scanty importance to tourism even though they virtually control the tourism product located within their boundaries. They are responsible, interlay, for local infrastructure, transport systems, sanitation and hygiene, leisure and recreation, law and order, the upkeep of local monuments and the general well-being of the tourist. Their support and participation is essential for tourism to succeed and spread its benefits among the host population. Their lack of interest has resulted in an unprofessional ad hoc approach that acts as a deterrent to the growth of tourism. The approach of the state governments needs to be focused, highly professional and result-oriented if India is to avail of the opportunity that the currently favorable market trends have to offer.

Being a long haul destination, Delhi is more conveniently accessible by air and cannot be easily reached by rail or road. A restrictive air transport policy has a very deleterious effect on tourist traffic. There are insufficient connections to most tourism destinations. The situation could be eased if the large number of regional airports could open up as international airports. The existing international and national airports also require improvement. The price of aviation turbine fuel needs to be lowered to make air transport competitive and affordable. Today, it is cheaper to travel by air to neighboring countries from India than to travel to certain parts of India itself. A more liberal aviation bilateral regime and a new aviation policy to benefit the economy of the country as a whole rather than the national carriers alone would greatly aid the development of tourism. Central and state governments need to evolve a taxation regime, which is revenue generating without being burdensome. Accommodation and transport taxes tend to be very heavy in certain states while the excise policy in others is extremely harsh. The land policy in some states makes the setting up of a hotel a formidable exercise and as many as 48 clearances are required for the construction and running of a hotel. Such policies deter private sector investment. The importance of protecting private investment in tourism must also be appreciated and activities such as mining, unauthorized construction, encroachments and haphazard development around tourist resorts must be prevented through appropriate legislation and public support. A liberal travel and tourism policy of both the Central as well as the State governments will help to see Delhi a better tourist spot.

A major impediment to the growth of tourism in Delhi has been the lack of awareness about the benefits that it can bestow upon the host population. Unless the host population, both in the rural and urban Delhi areas, is supportive of tourism, it cannot become a vibrant economic force. The rural sector, in particular, has been largely ignored in tourism development and has consequently been deprived of the benefits of employment and income generation accruing from tourism. The Next Plan will seek to rectify this, particularly in view of the world-wide interest in rural tourism. While an awareness campaign that elicits local support for travel and tourism is essential for the long-term growth of the sector, it is also important to create awareness about the environmental impact of tourism by generating respect for the carrying capacities of tourist destinations. This is imperative as excessive exposure of ecologically fragile areas to human interference can lead to irreparable environmental degradation. As the demand for ecotourism is expected to grow enormously in the next decade, it is important to have regulations in place to prevent such damage. The local population must be convinced of the need to support such regulations in the interest of long-term sustainability. India's hill resorts have already suffered seriously from a lack of concern for their carrying capacities and the unchecked influx of tourists during the summer months. If India's forest sanctuaries and pristine beaches are not to suffer the same fate, attention will have to be paid during the

Tenth Plan to obtaining regulatory and public support for sustainability concerns. Delhi / New Delhi have also its tourist majors that need to be given urgent attention for their proper management.

Indian Tourism and Human Trafficking

While the international tourism industry has acknowledged the problem of pedophilia to a certain extent, their counterparts in India are yet to pay any heed to the problem. Tourism has been given the status of an industry in India. Tourism is seen to be a prime source of foreign exchange and a panacea to all the economic ills of a developing country. Most of the States have incorporated tourism in their development strategies. Beaches are being thrown open to tourism. Special Tourism Areas are being demarcated in the most environmentally sensitive region - the coastal region of India. The economic arguments in favour of tourism development have led policy-makers into ignoring the social costs associated with tourism. The National Women's Commission has found that Bangalore is one of the five major cities, which supplies 80 percent of the child prostitutes in the country. Based upon this finding, when the Karnataka State Commission for Women tried to investigate it further, they stumbled upon a major smuggling gang whereby girls from impoverished rural families were lured to Goa and pushed into the flesh trade. The coastal areas in Calangute, Candolin and Baga in Goa have been converted into a pedophiles' paradise. Kovalam in Kerala, Mahabalipuram in Tamilnadu are also following in the same footsteps.

While efforts are being made by NGOs and the Women's Commission to address the issue adequately, the Law enforcing agencies are still pretending to be ignorant of the presence of child Sexual abuse in India.

The issue of Pedophilia gained prominence in India only after the arrest of Freddy Peats in 1991. He was charged with forcing boys into homosexual activities and for possessing drugs and pornographic material. Freddy Peats who claims to be an Anglo-Indian has been a resident of Goa for over a decade. Investigations, after his arrest, revealed that Peats had been operating a pedophile den where boys between 6-16 years were forced into prostitution catering mainly to German tourists.

Tourism 2020 Vision

Tourism 2020 Vision is the World Tourism Organization's long-term forecast and assessment of the development of tourism up to the first 20 years of the new millennium which appraised the future of the WTO industry in the twenty first century and forecasts the sustainable growth for the next two decades. An essential outcome of the *Tourism 2020 Vision* is quantitative forecasts covering a 25 years period, with 1995 as the base year and forecasts for 2010 and 2020. Although the evolution of tourism in the last few years has been irregular, UNWTO maintains its long-term forecast for the moment. The underlying structural trends of the forecast are believed not to have significantly changed. Experience shows that in the short term, periods of faster growth (1995, 1996, 2000) alternate with periods of slow growth (2001 to 2003). While the pace of growth till 2000 actually exceeded the *Tourism 2020 Vision* forecast, it is generally expected that the current slowdown will be compensated in the medium to long term.

Source WTO

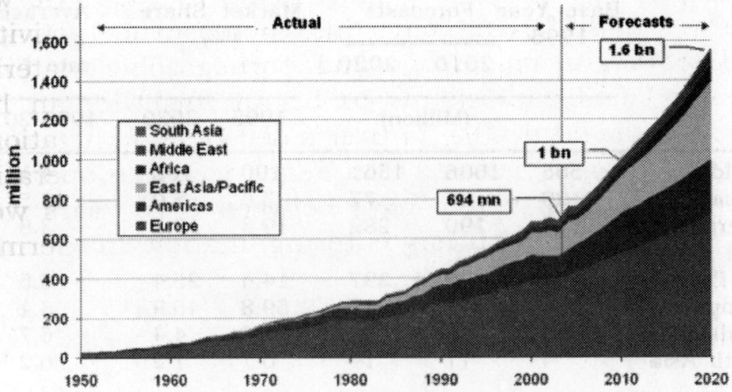

Source: WTO

UNWTO's *Tourism 2020 Vision* forecasts that international arrivals are expected to reach nearly 1.6 billion by the year 2020. Of these worldwide arrivals in 2020, 1.2 billion will be intraregional and 378 million will be long-haul travelers. The total tourist arrivals by region shows that by 2020 the top three receiving regions will be Europe (717 million tourists), East Asia and the Pacific (397 million) and the Americas (282 million), followed by Africa, the Middle East and South Asia. East Asia and the Pacific, Asia, the Middle East and Africa are forecasted to record growth at rates of over 5% year, compared to the world average of 4.1%. The more mature regions Europe and Americas are anticipated to show lower than average growth rates. Europe will maintain the highest share of world arrivals, although there will be a decline from 60 per cent in 1995 to 46 per cent in 2020. **(Source WTO)**

Long-haul travel worldwide will grow faster, at 5.4 per cent per year over the period 1995-2020, than intraregional travel, at 3.8 per cent. Consequently the ratio between intraregional and long-haul travel will shift from around 82:18 in 1995 to close to 76:24 in 2020.

	Base Year 1995	Forecasts 2010	2020	Market Share (%) 1995	2020	Average growth rate (%) 1995-2020
		(Million)				
World	565	1006	1561	100	100	4.1
Africa	20	47	77	3.6	5.0	5.5
Americans	110	190	282	19.3	18.1	3.8
East Asia and the Pacific	81	195	397	14.4	25.4	6.5
Europe	336	527	717	59.8	45.9	3.1
Middle East	14	36	69	2.2	4.4	6.7
South Asia	4	11	19	0.7	1.2	6.2

Source: WTO

THE ROLE OF STATE MECHANISM

The Indian Government has on paper ratified and accepted the UN Convention on the Rights of the Child. Article 35 of the UN Convention on the Rights of the Child states that "all appropriate national, bilateral and multinational measures will be taken by the state to prevent abduction, sale, trafficking, and coercion to engage in unlawful sexual activity and forms of exploitation such as prostitution, pornographic performances". The convention also states that all children must receive the opportunity to discover their identity and realize their self worth in a safe and supportive environment. The intent and purpose of the UN Convention on the Rights of the Child have not been incorporated in any Government Policy that would put an end to child prostitution. India is not immune to the problems of tourism related development. Existing State mechanism have to acknowledge the enormity of the problem and the shortage of applicable laws addressing trafficking in girls and boys and other abuses typical of the sex industry. Greater political will, more effective enforcement and adequate allocation of resources are needed to give effect to the spirit and letter of existing laws and conventions, policies and programmes. If the Government is not implementing these, then it is covertly abetting in the exploitation of the child.

THE ROLE OF OTHER ACTORS

Here lies the role of other actors in addressing the issue adequately. It is not an easy task to procure facts and figures to understand the issue due to its disguised and shrouded forms. The role of Family, Educational Institutions, Local Governance and Media, particularly in the tourist areas where children are vulnerable to this abuse can not be ignored.

Family rears the child first, who as an infant enjoys a long period of dependency, and the family is the most effective initial agent to address the issue. Therefore it becomes important for the parents and elders to be sufficiently sensitized to understand the problem and act accordingly with sympathy and compassion.

Teachers and Educational Institutions should be sensitized and equipped to handle the problem. Educational institutions should create a friendly atmosphere for the students to feel free to speak of any aberrant behavior they experience outside or inside the campus. The platform to tackle the issue of child Prostitution effectively starts at the Panchayats, Municipalities and Corporations. They should foster close cooperation and coordination with NGOs and other interest groups to plan, implement and evaluate measures, coupled with campaigns to mobilize local people to fight against this evil of the Tourism Industry. The media should not shrug away from its responsibility of providing a platform for advocacy. There is a need for a continuous campaign to keep the issue alive. While the media, NGO's, Panchayats, Schools, Colleges and the Government are players...the issue will not be resolved till the people take it on.

Measures Taken For Tourism Promotion in New Delhi

Post-Independence, while critical issues like agriculture, infrastructure and power supply hogged the limelight, travel and tourism received step daughterly treatment, as it was deemed a 'luxury' – affordable by only a few. Not much has changed over the last four decades, and it seemed every time the industry gained some form of momentum despite the closed and protected economy, there was something lurking in the shadows to clip its wings. The introduction of FERA put a serious crimp in foreign investment in the country and the Emergency was yet another deterrent to the tourism movement. A look at the Five Year Plans shows that in the Third Plan (1961-1966) tourism got approx 4.001 crores, which 0.11% of the total Plan outlay was. In the Eighth Plan, (1992-1997) it was Rs 272 crores – still 0.11% of the total plan outlay. At this time, policy makers, industry representatives and opinion makers equated tourism with foreign visitors. To their way of thinking, it was the foreign visitor who occupied hotel accommodation, filled airline seats, frequented bars and restaurants and used recreation facilities. Plus, given the foreign exchange (forex) shortage, the foreign tourist was looked upon as Daddy Big-Bucks – with an almost endless supply of crisp foreign currency. And while key aspects of Indian tourism came to be tailored to the foreign visitor, the price mechanism too, came to be tied to overseas costs. However, Delhi/ New Delhi being the capital city has certain advantages over other metro and non-metro cities.

Hotel rates, food and beverages in hotels, handicrafts, etc, were priced at a level much higher than the economic standards prevalent in the country at the time. No way could our rupee-toting lads compete. Thus, for our fellow countrymen, travel was restricted to places of pilgrimage or going to one's native town to visit the family once a year. However, other South East Asian countries were on the ball soon enough when they realized the potential of tourism. Hong Kong, Singapore and Thailand dug in the infrastructure, developed detailed tourism plans and marketed them in glorious technicolour across the world. Ironically, today, Indian outbound tourism provides a sizeable chunk of tourist inflow into these countries.

The tourism industry began to swing in the mid-90s, with the liberalization of the economy, and with India ratifying the agreement to set up the WTO unit in India. Foreign investment in industry, foreign investment in airlines and foreign media got the country excited about the world "out there" and the guy with 50 channels at his disposal, found bikini-clad motivation on his 21 inch screen, to get out of his armchair and check out new destinations. The last decade of the last century alone, saw an increase by more than 100 million travelers in the domestic tourism segment – from 63.8 million visitors in 1990, to 176 million in 1999.

Recently, Indian government adopted a multi-pronged approach for promotion of tourism, which includes new mechanism for speedy implementation of tourism projects, development of integrated tourism circuits and rural destinations, special capacity building in the unorganized hospitality sector and new marketing strategy. A nation wide campaign, for creating awareness about the effects of tourism and preservation of our rich heritage & culture, cleanliness and warm hospitality through a process of training and orientation was launched during 2004-05. The aim was to rebuild that sense of responsibility towards tourists among Indians and re-enforces the confidence of foreign tourist towards India as a preferred holiday destination. More than 6500 taxi drivers, restaurant owners and guides trained under the programme. Government also took several other initiatives to promote Indian tourism industry and increased the plan allocation for tourism i.e. from Rs

325 crore in 2003-04 to Rs. 500 crore in 2004-05. Road shows in key source markets of Europe, Incredible India campaign on prominent TV channels and in magazines across the world were among the few steps taken to advertise Indian tourism. In addition a task force was set up to promote India as prominent health tourism destination. However, in order to attract more visitors, India still needs to upgrade its airports, roads and other infrastructure to global standards. Even with the recent surge, tourist arrivals are just a mere percentage of those in such popular Asian destinations like Bangkok and Thailand.

Development in Tourism Industry in New Delhi

India Tourism office at Tokyo won two International Awards in Tour Expo held at Daegu in Korea for excellent tourism promotion. Indian Pavilion won the Best Booth Design Award as well as Best Folklore Performance Award competing with major players in tourism such as China, Japan, Thailand, Malaysia and Canada. The theme of pavilion was the Buddhist pilgrimage in India. Multi promotional activities undertaken by Tokyo office drew a large crowd to India Pavilion, which added colours to the entire travel show. The Korea's leading newspapers published on the front page the Incredible India booth's photographs highlighting various aspects. The live Yoga performance and Indian traditional snacks at the pavilion were enjoyed very much by the visitors.

Commonwealth Games 2010, New Delhi

'See You in Delhi', was the message that the Indian contingent had for the world, during the closing ceremony of the 2006 Melbourne Commonwealth Games. In 2010, India is going to become the second developing nation ever, to host the Commonwealth Games (CWG), the third largest multi sport event in the world. New Delhi, which has earlier played host to the 1982 Asian Games, is preparing itself to amaze the world. The games have the ability to transform the city's urban landscape and at the same time may simply be an extremely expensive 'PR' exercise. Considering the Indian contingent spent Rs. 40 crores on getting the message, 'See You in Delhi', across at the closing ceremony of the Melbourne games in an 11-minute show, it might end up being just that. The challenge is to ensure that the potential of the games as a catalyst for change is harnessed.

The CWG is going to be the first mega-event hosted by the city since the 1982 Asian Games, a gap of nearly thirty years. Much has changed, and yet much has remained unchanged in this time. India is preparing to break out on the world scene as an economic superpower, and the games are a step in propelling India on to the world stage. Yet India is still a poor country, ranked 127 out of 177 in the Human Development Index (HDI), and therefore one must question the rationale of spending more than a billion dollars on a sporting event. Is it going to be simply an exercise in nationalism and politician supported patriotism or is it going to have some notable positive effects on the community, and if so what precisely?

Since 2003, when India won the bid to host the games, various agencies and government bodies have been hard at work making plans for the upcoming event. The over arching theme seems to be to make Delhi a 'world class' city by 2010. This of course is a task easier said than done in a city of nearly 15 million people, growing at a phenomenal pace, and largely in a haphazard manner. Urban renewal or regeneration has been a theme in many such events in the past and appears an important one in the 2010 games as well.

This is because it gives an opportunity to improve the infrastructure and appearance of the host city, and also gives global media exposure meaning that the image of a city can be transformed in the eyes of viewers. This was certainly true of Barcelona, which successfully rid itself of its traditional manufacturing city image when hosting the 1992 Olympics (Brown, A and Massey, J. 2001). Manchester used the 2002 Commonwealth games as a tool to revive East Manchester, formerly an industrial area that had been suffering low growth and degradation.7 The urban landscape Delhi too, is set to change dramatically with many infrastructure projects being pushed through in time for 2010.

In Delhi's bid for the games, it states that through the games, the city wishes to, among other things:

1. Stimulate economic growth and development.
2. Improve city infrastructure.

Thus two of the professed aims of the games are to improve the welfare of the citizens of the city through improving facilities and promoting investment in the city. The focus area of the games this time is going to be East Delhi, across the Yamuna, where the games village and some of the venues are to be located. Residents of the area are hoping for a similar transformation as the one South Delhi experienced in the run up to the 1982 games. Infrastructure investments have already increased dramatically in the region with a new bridge being built at Wazirabad, the metro phase 2 being constructed, and numerous flyovers and roads in the pipeline. There are indeed ambitious plans afloat ranging from improving street furniture to setting up more power stations before the 2010 deadline.

The work ahead of the games can be broadly grouped into the following:

1. New Stadiums and renovation of existing stadiums
2. Games Village.
3. Transport sector.
4. Urban infrastructure like water and electricity.

5. Efforts to make Delhi 'world-class'.

Originally the plan was to build a completely new athletics stadium, one that would outrival J.N. Stadium. However lack of funds and available land has meant that the organizing team has had to rein in its ambitions. Now the plan is to build one large new stadium, an aquatics centre in the Delhi University with five swimming pools, as well as a new TT hall in the Yamuna Sports Complex and new stadiums for Badminton and Squash in the

Siri-Fort Sports Complex. The project in DU, which is going to give a major boost to sports there, is to have an Olympic-size (50 meters) pool, a diving pool, pool for synchronized swimming, one for water polo and a warm-up pool as well as a gym. The university is also set to be the venue for the Rugby 7's event.

The existing stadiums are however going to need extensive renovation before they can match up to the standards of the CWG. As reported in the Indian Express, the work remaining on the existing stadia is extensive. The estimated expenditure, only for renovation work, is over Rs.1250 crores. (Ramachandran, R. 2006). An outline of the projected work is

National stadium

- To be made spectator-friendly, playing turf to be moved closer
- Rear seating gallery to make way for changing rooms, medical rooms, offices
- Three new turfs, with floodlight facilities at two, including main arena

Source: Common wealth Game Delhi

Indira Gandhi Indoor Stadium, Yamuna Velodrome

- Stadium roof to be changed
- AC, lighting, audio-visual systems to be replaced

- New warm-up gym on the Lakeside
- On eastern side, a hostel and multi-media center will be set up.
- Cycling velodrome will be upgraded.

Source: Common wealth Game Delhi

Nehru stadium

- Major upgrade for Games showpiece: from open-close roof (partial) with filament material to constructing a tunnel leading to players' warm-up area
- New floodlights (with the pillars inside), audio/ visual system to electronic scoreboard and partial AC
- All upper tiers will have bucket seats instead of existing concrete arrangement.
- Stadium will be linked with rail-road-metro system (Railway Ministry has been notified about this and it will have to undertake the job at its cost with a station close by).

Source: Common wealth Game Delhi

Talkatora pool

- Existing pool will be renovated completely (with AC possible) and covered
- New pool for synchronized swimming to be constructed.
- But the pools will be used for training purposes only.

Source: Common wealth Game Delhi

Karni Singh shooting range

A new 300-metre range and a Final Scoring System range—the finals of 10, 15 and 25 meters events will be held—will be constructed.

Though construction of new stadiums and up gradation of the existing ones is central to the run up to the Games, the CWG is after all a sporting event; it is by no means the only focus area. Delhi is attempting to give itself a major facelift due to the games, and develop a whole portion of the city, East Delhi and the Yamuna riverfront, which until now has been largely neglected. As Delhi expands rapidly and space runs out, the until now undeveloped Yamuna riverfront, largely inhabited by slum dwellers and vegetable growers, is looking like prime real estate. The banks of the Yamuna are the largest open space left in the city, as well as the largest groundwater recharge zone. The 25 km stretch along the river has 97 sq km of prime land, 7 per cent of Delhi's total area (Sethi, A. 2005). DDA and other government authorities seem to have big plans for the area, developing the banks as green spaces and commercial areas. The proposals are centered on a "Thames-type Plan", channeling the river and reclaiming the land for other uses. A first step in the development of the region is the Games Village, a mammoth Rs. 955 crore project being built on a 63.5-hectare site by the DDA, for the 8000 plus athletes and officials expected for the event. The land has already been acquired from UP at a cost of Rs. 19 Crore and the project is in the planning stage (Vishnoi, A. 2006). The village will of course not be a one off structure, but will need extensive transport links, amenity providers and so on. There are also eight to nine hotels planned for the area, which will in turn give rise to other auxiliary services coming up. The village will be a well-planned site, with facilities for recreation, commercial activities, hospitals, training, shopping and living, all at hand. Interestingly, one proposal for post event usage is to hand over the village to the Delhi University as hostels, as DU is facing a tremendous shortage of hostel space. This however seems to have run into rough weather with high costs involved and the DDA now seeming to prefer selling the units as mid income housing post games. Housing too is to get as shorten the arm with over 40,000 low-income housing units to be built before the 2010 games.

All this means rampant development of an area that is ecologically fragile and not suited for urban development. Already large structures like the Akshardham Temple, the power plants and the Delhi Secretariat encroach on the riverbed. It is thought to be unadvisable to construct on the riverbed as the area is low-lying and has sandy alluvial soil. Also the region is the city's largest groundwater recharge zone and rampant construction in the area would hamper this considerably. An integral part of the long-term plan for the river area is the channeling of the Yamuna. Many environmentalists however see this as a recipe for disaster. As Amita Baviskar points out "the Yamuna is neither the Thames nor the Seine. Its distinctive rhythm is harmonised to the Indian subcontinent's seasons. With the bulk of its flow concentrated in the monsoons, the Yamuna is liable to breach its embankments if denied its present fertile expanse." (Baviskar, A 2005) Recent events in New Orleans point to the dangers involved with constructing levees and embankments to build on low-lying areas.

In a move to ready the area for development, 'illegal' structures in the area are being demolished. This means that the slums that have spread in the area have to go, regardless of the fact that low-income housing is practically non-existent in the city and the slum dwellers are getting no relocation. The numbers can only be said to be frightening, in the last three years as many as 300,000 people have been evicted across New Delhi on top of the 280,000 who are being chased away from Yamuna banks. Many people point out the obvious elitism in these moves, with structures like the Delhi

Metro Depot, I.T. Park, near Shastri Park and the Akshardham Temple having to face no such problems, all sites which began construction before the Delhi government issued a `Public Notice for Change of Land Use'. (Sethi, A. 2005) Others like Dunnu Roy also point out that the reason for which these slums are ostensibly being removed, polluting the river, is illogical as these slums do not even receive enough water to be polluting the river.

The hospitality sector is another area that is estimated to grow rapidly in the coming years, with the help of the Commonwealth Games. The games are estimated to result in a large increase in demand for hotel rooms, with one estimate putting the requirement at 30,000 rooms for 2010. DDA is planning on auctioning over 20 sites for hotels, many in the vicinity of the games village. This would not only add about 7500 rooms, but also raise hundred's of crores for DDA. As of now there are only 6,500 rooms available in the star category hotels and about 7,000 rooms in the budget category. Surrounding states are also preparing to cash in with UP planning on having over 5000 rooms ready before 2010.

The transport sector has recently been getting a lot of attention in the last few years as the Delhi government has made it one of their aims to develop an effective mass transport system in the city, and solve the massive congestion problem that the city faces. This emphasis is only set to increase with the games arriving soon. The plans are enormous; flyovers, bypasses, broader roads, a larger metro system, an integrated Rail Bus Transport system, a High Capacity Bus system, an electric trolley bus system and a Light Rail Transit system are all in the pipeline. (Roy, S. 2006) The transport sector has already been assigned the lion's share of the Tenth Plan outlay, at 23.68% of Rs. 23000 Crore.

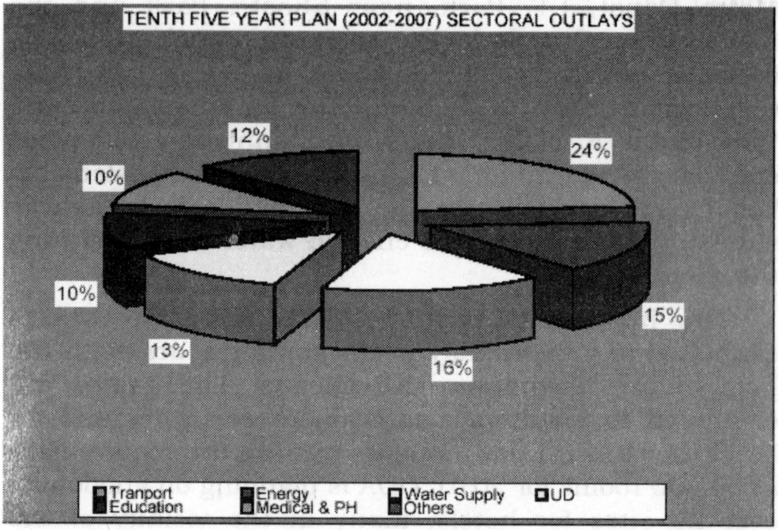

The transport infrastructure planned to be in place before 2010 is enormous. 25 new flyovers and underpasses are being planned at an estimated cost of Rs. 1650 Crores. These flyovers are to be largely concentrated in East and South Delhi, as well as on the ring roads so to make them signal-free. An underground tunnel road is also in the pipeline, connecting the J.N. stadium with the Games Village. A new bridge over the Yamuna, at Wazirabad, is almost in the construction stage, with the plans for the Rs. 464 crores project ready. The bridge is at the centre of the regeneration plans that the city government has for the Yamuna area. It is to be the city's first hanging bridge and ready in time for the 2010 Games.

The roads of the city are to get a major facelift before the games with many bypasses and broadening projects planned. Roads like the Mehrauli-Mahipalpur Road, Mehrauli-Badarpur Road and interconnecting roads which link up to the airport are to be broadened. Along with this, roads, which interlink the various stadia, and around major tourist attractions are also to be improved at a cost of nearly Rs. 170 crores. Two bypasses are also planned at a cost of around Rs 30 crores (Roy, S. 2006). Another ambitious project is to develop a third ring road, which will actually encircle Delhi state. This 'peripheral expressway' is projected to be 270 km long, with a 136-km Western Peripheral Expressway and a 134-km Eastern Peripheral Expressway, and will go through large parts of Haryana, UP and Delhi. This will dramatically reduce pressure on Delhi's existing ring roads, as at the moment inter-state traffic has no way of bypassing the city. This project, which was floated nearly a decade ago, has got a new lease of life with the 2010 Games around the corner, and construction is under way(Joshi, S 2005).The maintenance of the two ring roads has also, for the first time, been handed over to private companies.

The emphasis of the present Rapid Transport system is now on the Metro. The metro, whose presentation before the Commonwealth Games evaluation team made a sizable impression, is at the core of developing an efficient mass transport system in the city with Phase 1 of the metro being fully operational. However more importantly, phase 2, aimed at extending the network much further in the city, is already under construction, and is set to be ready before 2010. This phase is going to require massive investment, over Rs 8000 crores. (Chatterjee M. B. 2006) The second phase is going to provide a vital transport link to East Delhi, with a dedicated Games Village station. (See map) The metro, which is already beginning to have an impact on the city's congested roads, will be able to make a much larger impact as its network and reach grows. The second phase, originally planned to be ready by 2010-2011 is now going to be operational by 2009, due to the 2010 Games. The new line may even extend up to the airport in time for the Games. Other transport sector improvements slated for 2010 are 98 km of High Capacity Bus system, 32 km of electric trolley bus system, a Light Rail Transit system, 1,000 quality Radio taxis at airports and major railway stations, 200 new AC buses and 100 mini-buses for athletes, managers and officers and 800 deluxe buses for park-and-ride services for spectators. There are also plans afoot to set up three smaller ISBT's in the city. One of the most important improvements is to be the newly privatized airport. This point is enumerated on further, later in the paper.

The impact that the Games has on providing basic amenities to the city is crucial to how the city's citizens will view the games. It may not be the size of the stadiums or the number of flyovers that are built which will decide whether the games find a place in Delhi'ites hearts; it may be relatively less glamorous things like water, electricity, sanitation and solid waste management. In recent years Delhi has been reeling under a severe water and power shortage, and if the Games are able to expedite movement in these sectors, the citizens of Delhi will be the gainers.

The summer of 2006 saw one of the worst shortages of power in recent history with the government even attempting to clamp down on usage by homes, shops and commercial establishments. The peak power consumption this summer was 3725 MW; during the Commonwealth Games in 2010, consumption is estimated to be over 7000 MW, nearly double of this year's peak.(Joshi, S. 2005b) The government has already got two large new power plants in the pipeline, slated to be ready in time for the Games. However even with these in place, total production of power in Delhi will only reach a maximum capacity of 2300 MW, leaving a shortfall of at least 4700 MW. The two new plants, one in Bawana and the other, an extra unit being added to the existing Pragati plant, are both Gas based, and will add 1000MW and 300 MW respectively to Delhi's production capacity. The present production is dependant on four power plants, The Indraprastha power plant, the Raj Ghat power plant, the Gas Turbine plant and Pragati power plant. However with the exception of the Pragati plant, which is only four years old, none of the plants can produce anywhere close to capacity due to outdated and ill maintained equipment. This makes the city heavily dependent on the Northern Grid for power. The Northern Grid is however already over burdened, supplying electricity to numerous northern states including Uttar Pradesh, Uttaranchal, Haryana, Punjab and Rajasthan. This might lead to a situation of FHB (Family Hold Back) as Jug Suraiya humorously points out in his article 'Bhago Dilli'.

So all the bijli available, little as it might be, will be diverted from unessential consumers such as hospitals, schools, workplaces and private homes and given to foreign visitors. And if all this diverted bijli proves insufficient, extra supplies can be obtained from neighbouring areas like Gujarat, Madhya Pradesh, Tamil Nadu and the Andaman and Nicobar Islands."(Suraiya, J. 2006)

This, though exaggerated, may be quite an accurate picture of the situation sans 2010. Delhi's 'world-class' city status will be at stake, and to achieve this, it may be necessary to take some radical steps. The Games will have a very direct impact on power consumption, and we must see whether we are willing to pay the price for hosting the games, with others spending some nights in the dark.

Water is another problem very fast taking on crisis proportions. The city has one of the highest per capita water supplies in the world, at over 220 liters per person, per day. Yet water shortages are a perennial problem due to lack of accountability and the fact that they lose about 50 percent of available water. (Yadav, S. 2006) There is talk of improving water distribution systems before the 2010 games, a much-needed development for the city's citizens. New pipes will be laid in the area of the village to ensure better distribution. Water supply at stadia will also be upgraded along with and a new water treatment plant at the Games village (to treat a million gallons of water per day. Sanitation and sewerage, is also to be upgraded, and a dedicated sewage treatment plant constructed at the village

Solid waste management is another area where work has already begun to prepare the city. Waste management has been privatized in 6 of the 12 MCD zones already and 4 of the remaining 6 will also be privatized shortly. This step should be able to provide better quality, and save MCD money in the process.

The Delhi Government is also planning on making provisions for more toilets in public spaces. "Better quality public toilet facilities on all major roads, markets, public places will be provided by PWD, MCD & NDMC on BOT basis before Commonwealth Games, 2010."1

A large newspaper in the city recently ran a much publicized campaign called, 'From Walled City to World City.' The city seems to have begun a concerted effort to achieve what is known in the media as 'global standards.' In this effort there are numerous steps being taken to transform the face of the city, from better street lighting, to sleeker bus shelters to upgrading the airport. This effort is resulting in over Rs. 100 Crore being spent on street furniture and landscaping alone.(Roy, S. 2006) This will give the city a much needed facelift in terms of utilities like bus shelters, dust bins, street lighting and park benches.

The other major boost to infrastructure is the airport privatization. In 1982, a new International Departure and Arrival hall had been built. This time, after a stringent bidding process, the government formally privatized the entire airport, with the GMR 15 Delhi airport passenger handling capacity to treble New Delhi,

May 18, 2006

http://www.hindustantimes.com/news/181_1700709,00020016.htm

group winning the bid. The airport is now set for an overdue modernization plan with capacity to treble, from 10 million to 35 million, by 2010.This is an essential step towards improving connectivity within India and with the rest of the world, and will also play a determining role in the number of tourists who finally come to Delhi for the 2010 Games.

The attempts to make Delhi a 'world class' city however has a darker side as it also means that a large number of marginalized people are further marginalized as they do not fit into the larger scheme of things. Demolitions of slums in the Yamuna pushta area have become increasingly commonplace with the site for the Games Village being in the vicinity. Over six lakh hawkers may also face evacuation before the games (Afsal, M 2005). Migrant labour, which entered the city in lakhs in 1982, will probably have to face similar deplorable conditions this time around too. They are needed for the ambitious construction projects envisaged but will have to be kept out of sight, as their conditions would not be in sync with that of a world-class city like Delhi. It is extremely important to ensure that these games do not simply give added benefits to those who are already privileged, but also attempt to aid the marginalized, not further worsen their position.

The infrastructure developments that the city needs, will mean investments of over a billion dollars, not including the amount being spent on projects like the metro, airport and peripheral expressway. This is more than three times the estimate that the IOA had made in its bid for the games, which was under 300million dollars. Like any such event, there are a number of agencies involved, at last count over 45. There are however four primary organizations co coordinating the work. A rough breakup of expenditure between these organizations is shown in the pie chart below:

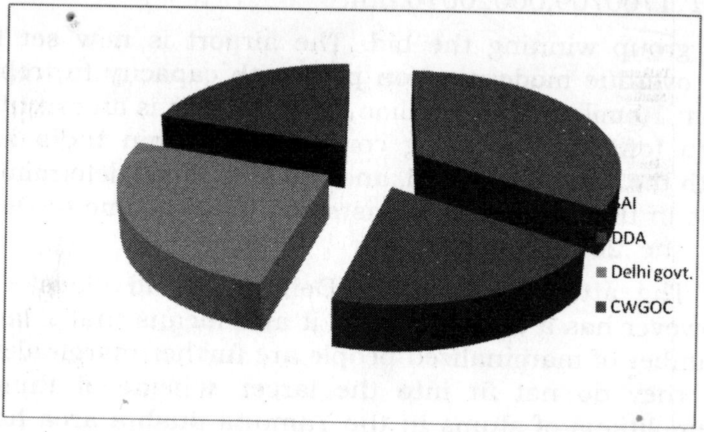

Figures in Crores

The Delhi government has asked for Rs 1,314 crore for creating infrastructure, flyovers, new roads and to find a solution to Delhi's chaotic traffic.

DDA has to build the athletes' village and the new stadiums at Siri Fort Sports complex and the Yamuna sports complex, and have asked for Rs.983 crore.

The Sports Authority of India has asked for the biggest chunk of Rs 1,700 crore to renovate all existing stadiums as they are in a bad shape and need an urgent makeover. SAI also needs to build a few more stadiums.

The organizing committee, which has asked for Rs.980 crores will be spending Rs 200 crore for conducting the games, Rs100 crore for the opening and closing ceremonies, Rs 100 crore for equipment, Rs 50 crore for the expenses at the games village, Rs 40 crore for the media center, Rs 45 lakh to be paid to each of the 71 countries as part of the training expenses.

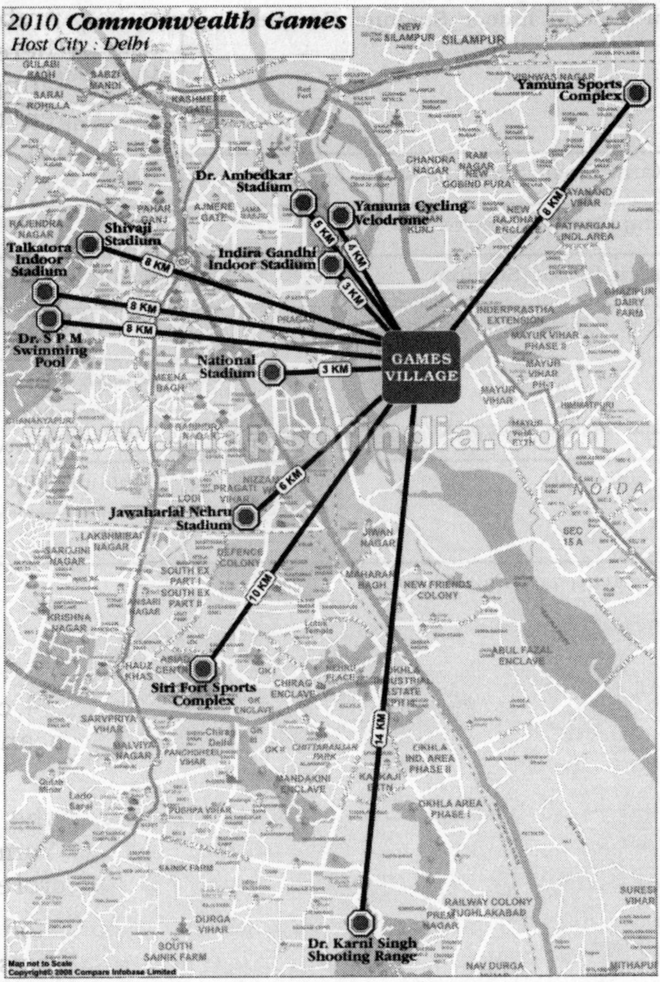

Venues by MAP

Jawaharlal Nehru Stadium	Athletics
	Lawn bowls
	Weightlifting
Maj. Dhyan Chand National Stadium	Hockey

Indira Gandhi Indoor Stadium Complex	Cycling
	Gymnastics
	Wrestling
Dr. Karni Singh Shooting Range	Shooting
Tyagaraj Sports Complex	Netball
Talkatora Indoor Stadium	Boxing
Siri Fort Sports Complex	Badminton
	Squash
Yamuna Sports Complex	Table tennis
Delhi University	Aquatics
	Rugby 7s

Source-www.cwgdelhi2010.com

2

OBJECTIVES OF THE STUDY

The study on consumer protection in the travel and tourism industry in India revolves around the following broad objectives:-

- ❖ To study the Tourism and travel industry in Delhi, its evolution and growth with special reference to the barriers of tourism growth in New Delhi (India).
- ❖ To study the Promotion campaigns carried out by DTDC, Tour Operators, Travel Agencies and Hotels to promote tourism in Delhi.
- ❖ To list the various Promotional Activities undertaken by various Tourist Destinations in Delhi.
- ❖ To study the various promotional tools used in promoting Tourism in Delhi
- ❖ To study the consumers' problems in the tourism industry and possible effective measures that can be taken for protection of consumers' interests.
- ❖ To give an analytical picture of the issue of consumer protection in the travel and tourism industry in New Delhi

Objectives (what)

- To develop, endorse and disseminate codes of conduct for visitors and tour operators
- To raise awareness of visitors and tour operators about the consequences of their behavior and seek cooperation to prevent negative tourism impact and encourage conservation behavior in protected areas by self regulation measures

Codes of conduct must be effectively distributed to visitors and tour operators. They can be printed on brochures, exhibited on signs where they are easily seen, and/or proclaimed verbally to visitors by staff or local guides. Codes of conduct for visitors are most useful when made available on site. If visitors can actually see the impact of inappropriate conduct or experience the fragility of protected area resources immediately after reading a code of conduct, the do's and don'ts will come to life. Awareness and knowledge about the consequences of their behavior can induce visitors to adopt a code of conduct that would help to minimize impact and/ or take part in conservation. In addition, social and economic incentives can be effective instruments to encourage voluntarily adoption of a code of conduct. The process of developing a tourism code of conduct should begin by forming a taskforce within the protected area management for the purpose of drafting the code. The taskforce should then seek further input from other stakeholders such as the private sector and non-governmental organizations through an intensive consultative process. When developing a code of conduct for protected areas, all environmental, social, and economic aspects should be included. A code of conduct for visitors is most useful when made available on site. Effective ways to disseminate information which can enhance knowledge and raise the awareness of visitors are, for instance, pre-orientation sessions before the start of tourism activities, distribution of well-designed brochures at park entrances, displaying information on how to be good to the environment and be culturally sensitive in protected areas, and making this available in visitor centers and tourism locations. Distribution of the code of conduct to a wide-spread audience can be done in cooperation with public/mass media such as television, travel magazines, etc.

The Indian Consumer Protection Act, 1986 was enacted "to provide for better protection of the interests of consumers and for that purpose to make provision for the establishment of consumer councils and other authorities for the settlement of consumers disputes and for matters connected therewith"1. The obvious objective is to protect consumers from exploitation. The Act was last amended in 2002, which came into effect on 15th March, 2003. It applies to all goods and services unless specifically exempted by the Government. Until now no sector has been specifically exempted and, therefore, it is universally applicable.

Consumer's categories

The basic purpose of the Act is to provide relief to four categories of persons, viz.

- Consumers, who have purchased goods for consideration, if they suffer from any defect;
- Consumers from whom the trader has charged a price in excess of the price displayed on the goods or package thereof or price list exhibited, or as agreed between the parties or the one fixed under any law;
- Consumers who have suffered loss or damage as a result of any unfair trade practice or unscrupulous exploitation by the trader; and
- Consumers of service for consideration, if it suffers from deficiency in any respect."

The Act also provides for a three tier redressed mechanism for consumer grievances, consisting of the District Forum, the State Commission and the National Commission. Pecuniary limits for original jurisdiction for the three redressed agencies have been prescribed by the Act. While the legislation is at the national level the administration at the district and state levels has been left to various States governments who have framed rules in this regard. The National Commission is constituted by the central government and has the power to make its own rules. The National Commission also has the power to review its order. Appeals from the District for lie to the respective State Commission and from State Commission to the National Commission. Appeal against the orders of the National Commission, in case of original jurisdiction; lie to the Supreme Court of India. As regards orders passed by the Commission in its appellate or revisonal capacity there is no provision for appeal.

The three tier Redressed Authorities are quasi-judicial Tribunals. Their decisions can be appealed only in the manner laid down in the Act and cannot be agitated in a Civil Court. They are vested with the power: to give „cease and desist order ; to order issue of corrective advertisement to neutralize the effect of the impression created by the misleading advertisement; to provide adequate cost to the parties; to grant ad interim stay or injunction; and to award compensation; and to order compensation to be paid by public servants for their mala fide, oppressive or capricious act, where circumstances so warrant. The provisions of the Consumer Protection Act, 1986 are in addition to and not in derogation of any other law. The Redressed forums at the District level have power to pass interim order, as is just and proper.

Consumer protection generally involves compensation for the loss cr damage suffered by the consumer.

Competition law goes beyond this and ensures that the market functions efficiently. Consumers other than those immediately affected and who have complained would also benefit. Besides, the definition of consumer under the consumer protection law and that under Competition Act, 2002 differ. Commercial buyers stand excluded from the definition of consumers under consumer protection law, but not under the Competition law. Consumer protection law and Competition law are currently administered by two separate Ministries in the Government of India. Their respective policies are also, therefore, formulated separately, but process of consultation is provided in government business rules. The MRTP Act, 1969 is still in vogue and has under its purview UTPs which consist of: misrepresentation and false or disparaging advertisement; deceptive practices; lucky draw; violation of standards; and destruction of goods, with a view to affecting price. MRTP Commission thus dispenses partly consumer protection, though except for the UTPs the rest of the consumer redresses are under the Consumer Protection Act, 1986.

There is strong commonality between competition policy and law on the one hand and consumer protection policy and law on the other. An effective competition policy lowers entry and exit barriers and makes the environment conducive to promoting entrepreneurship, which also provides space for the growth of small and medium enterprises and consequent employment expansion. Competition law concentrates on maintaining the process of competition between enterprises and tries to remedy behavioral or structural problems in order to re-establish effective competition on the market. The consequence of this is higher economic efficiency, greater innovation and enhancement of consumer welfare. Thereby the consumer experiences wider choice and greater availability of goods at affordable prices. On the other hand, the consumer protection policy and law are primarily concerned with the nature of consumer transactions, trying to improve market conditions for effective exercises of consumer choice. Thus, the two disciplines focus on different market failures and offer different remedies, but are both aimed at maintaining well functioning, competitive markets that promote consumer welfare. The two disciplines are mutually reinforcing. Voluntary adoption of a code of conduct by tour operators can be motivated by offering them an incentive for being the tour operator with the most appropriate behavior. The management of the protected area publishes and distributes its code of conduct to the tour operators in national parks. Then an evaluation system for awarding the "best conducted" tours with respect to the established code of conduct must be developed. Awards or emblems for being the "best tour operator" given by the area management can be used as a powerful motivational tool for that tour operator since most people are now conscious about caring for the environment. Protected area management or marketing authorities could choose to promote or suggest specific tour operators who have eagerly adopted the code of conduct and could black-list those who are insensitive to it (IUCN, 1996). Organizational arrangements endorsing the code of conduct as a requirement for tourism management should guarantee the commitment of managers towards a code of conduct which encompasses the environmental, social, and economic aspects of sustainable tourism in protected areas. Besides, a planning instrument that emphasize multi-sectoral consulting procedures should ensure high standard codes of conduct which can diminish the impact of tourism on the park environment, and promote sustainable socio-economic conditions. Economic instruments can play an important role in the response of tour operators who realize they could either receive an award or risk being black-listed.

CONSUMER PROBLEMS IN THE TOURISM SECTOR IN DELHI

India's outbound market experienced a 64% growth between 2001 and 2006, increasing from 4.6 million outbound travellers to 7.5 million outbound travellers. This expansion coincides with the rapid economic development that India has been experiencing. As a popular destination for outsourced work, India's economic landscape has been changing rapidly with a new middle class rising. However, given the changes in attitudes and behaviors in the Indian market, current destination trends are not guaranteed to remain fixed as the outbound market continues to expand.

Indian Outbound Travellers - Thousands

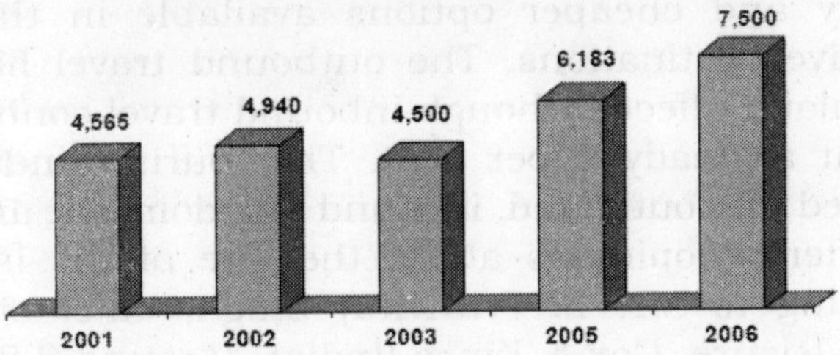

Source: Euromonitor Estimates, via Tourism Australia (2006 projected by Insignia from available data)

As with other origin markets, the motivations to travel to mid-haul destinations are generally escape/relaxation related:

- Shopping
- Nightlife
- Spas
- Beaches
- Fun

The Indian Travel and tourism industry in Delhi is going through trying times because of the general global recession, uncertainty in the political scenario of the

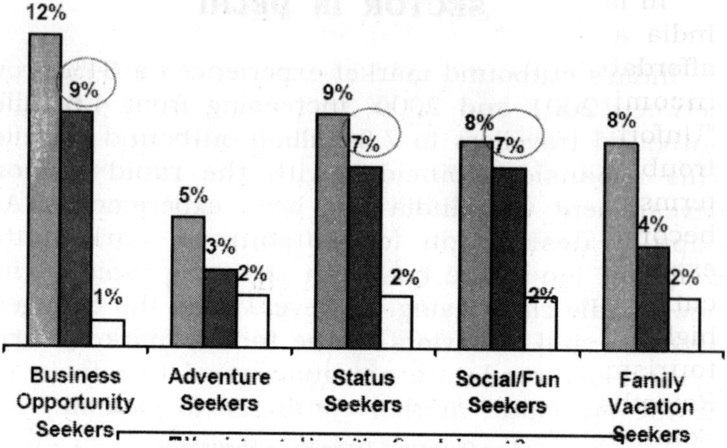

country and cheaper options available in the other attractive destinations. The outbound travel has been particularly affected though inbound travel continues to grow at a steady 6 per cent. The tourism industry is classified into outbound, inbound and domestic and there are different opinions about the size of the industry. According to Mr. L. Prithviraj Singh, chief operating officer, leisure, Cox & Kings (India), "Around 2.5 million tourists are coming in while outbound is still a nascent market. The potential for growth in the latter segment is much more than for incoming tourists." Mr. Sunil Gupta, head, leisure travel, Thomas Cook (India), said, "Inbound tourism is growing at a consistent CAGR of 6 per cent annually while outbound tourism is growing at 15 per cent year-on-year. Mr. Ranjit Malkani, chairman and managing director, Kuoni Travel India (KTIL), at a recent press gathering, said there was a definite slowdown in outbound travel. Further, "Growth in inbound travel so far has been due to tourists from West Asia, Latin America and Japan. The trend in European arrivals has been flat, though a 5-6 per cent growth is expected courtesy the rise in airline seat capacity."

In fact, the recent rise in airline seating capacity to India and increase in hotel rooms have spelt greater affordability for the foreign traveller. But Mr. Singh said incoming traffic has grown only marginally. "Unfortunately, foreign agents look upon India as a troublesome country - in terms of operations not in terms of safety. We have also got into this trap of India becoming an expensive destination - added to an expensive air fare - as there is 'no open sky' policy. The entry points are the metros where hotel tariffs are very high. Basic infrastructure too is a problem." Inbound tourism is concentrated largely in the North and Rajasthan. Industry sources say that even today, the South accounts for only about 25 per cent of inbound tourism. "The first time traveller will invariably go to Agra and Rajasthan and not venture to other locales." However, added Mr. Singh, "with the thrust given by Kerala, it is an exotic option and Gujarat too is a destination of the future." Domestic tourism needs to be buoyed up. "Domestic tourists are looking at 3-4 holidays in a year in India and the concept of booking through a hotel directly is moving away and customers are increasingly coming to travel and tour agencies." said Mr. Singh. The most favoured destinations continue to be the hill stations and Rajasthan and now, with the marketing thrust, Kerala is the largest destination for people in the West and South.

"One has to really bring tourism to its potential. We have not even scratched the surface. The need is to evolve a long term policy. Disinvestment of Government stake in Indian Airlines, Air India and ITDC in the long term will be a good thing and if ITDC hotels are privatized, that will open up a new level of affordable hotels." said Mr. Singh, adding, "The problem in India is the absence of 'open sky' policy. If there is one, prices will drop, capacities will improve and once that happens, all the other problems will be sorted out." Among the leading players, Kuoni Travel (India) (KTIL) is the countries biggest, fully owned by the Zurich-based Kuoni Travel Holding. Last week, the company acquired Tour Club which caters to the outbound segment from West Asia to India. Inbound travel from West Asia has been growing at 15 per cent, among the highest growth rates in the segment.

How the Tourism Industry Can Effectively Satisfy the Consumer

Tourism involves traveling to relatively undisturbed or uncontaminated natural areas with the specific objects of studying, admiring and enjoying the scenery and its wild flora and fauna, as well as other existing cultural and historical aspects. A visit with a motto to know these areas is nothing but tourism. Places of tourist interest are numerous and of varied nature. These include places of archeological and historical importance, pilgrimage centers, sanctuaries, national parks, hill resorts and sea beaches, etc. The paper has been prepared on the basis of the secondary published data which show that since 1950 the tourism industry of India is expanding. The number of foreign tourists have been increased to more than 21 lakhs by 2001. India has a minimal share of only 0.39% of the world tourism trade. India employs nearly 10 million people in this industry making it the second largest employer of the country. Recent political unrest, fear of violence, terrorism, strikes and epidemics etc. are detrimental to our tourism business. However, considering the recent development, it is hoped that India will get her due share in world tourism.

Marketing of Tourism Services include mainly the services sold to domestic and foreign tourists. The domestic tourism is an important segment of the overall tourist scenario although no reliable data are available in this regard. It is relatively easy to keep record of foreign tourists as they are registered at entry points like international airports which is not possible in case of domestic tourists. The number of domestic tourists, according to a rough estimate, was 348 million in 1987 which rose to 81 million in 1993 and over 100 million in 2001. Domestic tourism fosters a sense of unity in otherwise diverse environment of the country and contributes to national integration. Even if 10% of the population travels outside the native state, it involves a massive movement of nearly 10 crore people who develop the fillings that they are traveling within their own country. Larger income and longer holidays coupled with certain incentives given by public and private organizations to their workers, have contributed a lot in infusing interest to look around to a place for an annual or bi-annual visit with family members. Even though India has a very meager share amounting to 0.38 percent of tourists and 0.51 percent of the amount of world tourism trade in 2001, it has the hope for attracting more and more foreign tourists by exploiting her unexploited tourist spots of the country. Mostly tourists from North America, Central and South America, Africa, Australia, Western Europe, Eastern Europe, West Asia, South Asia, South East Asia and East Asia are visiting India as foreign tourists. Out of these the share of North America, Western Europe, West and South Asia occupies a major share in increasing Indian tourism trade. India accounts for four out of five tourists to South Asia. Another healthy trend in the foreign tourism in India since 1991 is the conspicuous increase in business travels with its spin off effects in up gradation of accommodation and introduction of new technology in communications and other services. On an average, a foreign tourist stays for about 27 days in India which is an important indicator of increase of the foreign exchange earned by the country.

Tourism in India has vast employment potential, much of which still awaits exploitation. At present about

8.5 million persons are directly employed by hospitality services. This is about 2.4 percent of the total work force of the country. In addition, the industry provides indirect employment to about 30 million persons. Further it is interesting to note that the employment generation in proportion to investment is very high in tourism industry. According to an estimate, an investment of Rs.10 lakh creates 89 jobs in hotels and restaurants sector as against 44.7 jobs in agriculture and 12.6 in manufacturing industry. Another important aspect of employment in tourism is that it employs a large number of women in hotels, airlines services, travel agencies, handicrafts making and marketing and cultural activity centers. As per 1983-84 indices the employment output ratio in tourism was 71, whereas in leather 51, textiles 27, electricity 14, beverages 12 and cement 6. Generally the visit of a foreign tourist to India provides employment to one person and 6.5 domestic tourists generate one job.

Hotel sector is the key segment of tourism industry to earn foreign exchange. Realizing the importance of hotel segment the government has taken initiatives to encourage hotel industry by providing tax benefits and other incentives. Foreign investment and collaboration are now facilitated under new economic policy. The hotel industry has shown a spectacular growth during the last one and half decades. The number of hotel rooms has increased from 30200 in 1986 to 57386 in 1995 and to 62000 in 1996 and to 68000 in 2001. In the approved list of Department of Tourism the classified hotels are 125 in One Star, 286 Two Star, 274 Three Star, 73 Four Star, 56 Five Star, 42 Five Star Deluxe, and 41 of heritage hotel category. In spite of rapid strides made by the hotel industry since last one decade or so, the hotel accommodation falls short of the requirement of growing inflow of the tourists. Assuming a modest growth rate of 7 to 8 percent per annum, the requirement to hotel rooms is expected to rise to 91,000 by 2002-03 and to 1.125 lakh rooms by 2005. Besides a large number of budget hotels will be required for about 200 million strong middle class Indian tourists also.

Places of tourist interest are so numerous and of varied nature that it is not easy to describe these places comprehensively. These include mostly the Himalayan Region, the great plain of north India, the peninsular plateau and coastal plains. In general the tourist spots are counted more like Buddhist sites, Shrines, Forts, places of historical importance, hot springs, Jain monasteries, lakes and birds, sanctuaries, religious centers, science spots, sea beaches, summer resorts, waterfalls and wild lives etc. In this context, a reference can be drawn for Orissa that all above kinds of spots are richly available to attract more and more foreign as well as domestic tourists.

Although Delhi has progressed a lot since the fifties with respect to tourism, she is still way behind the developed. India earns one seventh of China, one fourth of Indonesia and less than half of Philippines from tourism in comparison. Delhi is no exception to this. The development of tourism depends upon the development of an integrated infrastructure of national and international highways, railways, ports, civil aviation, telecommunication, hotel accommodation and allied services. Inadequacies of such infrastructural facilities adversely affect tourism. The sluggish growth of Delhi tourism arises from its inability to sell effectively her rich tourist potential. Delhi should market itself as a value added tourism destination stressing its variety and cost effectiveness. Satisfaction of the tourist should be the top priority of the tourist industry. Apart from infrastructural development, tourism requires an environment of peace and stability where the tourist is sure of his safety and security. Political unrest and fear of violence is a death knell to tourist industry. Unfortunately, one part or the other of the country is hit by bandhs, strikes, ethnic clashes and insurgency which adversely affect our tourism service marketing. Epidemics, such as plague, AIDS and dengue fever are also detrimental to the growth of tourism. It is surprising that some small countries like Malaysia, Indonesia, Hongkong and get Singapore have been able to attract more tourists and better receipts than India. Even in terms of quality, the diminutives like Maldives and Bhutan present an appreciable model of sustainable tourism. In this context, in order to give a Philip to the tourism trade the Central Government as well as the State Government should come forward to develop some of the newly unexploited and selected tourist places, diversify some of the culture oriented tourism to holiday and leisure tourism, develop trekking, winter sports, wild life, beach resorts tourism, launching, key markets near tourist centers, provide inexpensive accommodation and to improve service efficiency. India still hopes better to improve the tourism marketing services and to take an equal and more challenging steps with her competitors in the field more vigoursly. All these considerations need to be understood and steps may be taken accordingly for improvement of the travel and tourism industry in Delhi.

Hospitality Industry is closely linked with travel and tourism industries. A sudden boom in travel and tourism has led to the development of hospitality industry. And India experiencing huge footfalls as a favorite vacation destination of foreigners and natives is working towards improving its hospitality industry. Fierce competition and fight to rank on the number one position is leading leaders of this industry into contemplating innovative ideas and successful hospitality products and services every day. In fact some of the facts about hospitality industry in India can be explained on the basis of following points:

- Market choice
- Planned human resources management
- Employees training
- Market response
- Empowerment
- Behavior-based evaluation
- Marketing synergy
- Employee commitment
- Essential quality

However, to help hospitality industry in Delhi reach its height advance technologies and consumer favorable services are devised. Sitting at home a customer can reserve his/ her airline tickets and hotel rooms. This facility in the hospitality industry has surely brought revolutionary change.

The following key issues were used to help us focus the case study in order to address the central question: 'How are societal drivers – particularly tourism – impacting social ecosystems in the study area?'

- Population and population movements
- Occupational shifts
- Ecosystem or resource use
- Institutions
- Health of the ecosystem.

Population Movements

Out-migration created spaces for others to come in and also for alternative sources of income. On one hand, this created a new demand for land and, on the other, by reducing pressure on land due to out-migration, it made land available for conversion. In-migration was high soon after liberation in 1961, and then was positive but lower. The in-migrant creates a demand for land in part, but more important, he/she makes possible the continuation of services to agriculture (where necessary) or the introduction of new services such as those required by tourism. The tourist is also a temporary migrant creating his or her own set of demands in the area.

Shift from Primary Economic Activities

Over the four decades, there has been a steep fall in the percentage of population in the primary sector while the participation of the workforce in other sectors has increased. Adoption of New Resource Use Patterns: - Conversion from agricultural and orchard land into land for putting up buildings is common. Land is no longer central to the production process. A disjunction is observed between the social process and legal superstructure. While new progressive laws relating to agricultural lands were enacted to keep people in land and increase its productivity (GoG 1992a; 1992b), the strength of the demonstration effect arising from the high visibility of those engaged in the tertiary sector and the desire to cross class lines created pressures towards moving out of agriculture. Tourism and linked economic activity provide the opportunity.

Pressure on Local Institutions

The involvement of the local population in the main tourist villages is high at various levels, such as supplying goods and services to the industry, running hotels, and even providing land and housing to accommodate tourist infrastructure. However, the type and nature of involvement varies across the different types of establishments. There are enormous pressures on the central and state governments from hotel and builder lobbies (for construction permits) and on local governments–the Panchayats–from the local community (for permission to build in coastal areas).

Impact on the Eco-System

- ❖ Land use and cover changes
- ❖ Stress on coastal aquifers
- ❖ Degradation of coastal vegetation, with different implications for the health of the ecosystem.

3

RESEARCH METHODOLOGY

Mainly exploratory research would be carried out for both primary and secondary research. In order to accomplish the objectives of the study, it was essential to articulate the manner in which it is to be conducted, i.e., the research process is to be carried-out in a certain framework. The Research Methodology, which follows, is the backbone of the study.

Primary Research: Structured in-depth questionnaires would be used to probe individuals for information in the area which is being probed as the present problem of the study.

Secondary Research: Secondary data from different sources would be collected and used for certain aspects of research like operation of market strategies, their comparative advantages and their future prospects.

Tourism Policy

Tourism is the second largest net earner of foreign exchange in India generating about 3 billion dollars annually. Tourism has been given explicit attention through the Tourism Policy of 1982; the Report of the National Committee on Tourism, 1988; the National

Action Plan, 1992; and National Tourism Policy, 1998. The Seventh Five- Year Plan also proposed that tourism be declared an industry so that it could avail of the concessions available to industry. This decision was, however, left to the states, and not all have accepted. It also received an indirect boost through the rupee depreciation, which was part of the reform package as it made travelling to India that much cheaper and attractive. In the Eighth Five-Year Plan document, the importance of private sector participation in the future expansion of tourism is especially mentioned. The Plan directly addresses the 'local development' potential of tourism, by providing for the need of 'master plans' at the state level to integrate area plans with development of tourism.

The Ministry of Tourism is the nodal agency for the formulation of national policies and programmes and for the coordination of activities of various central and state government agencies and the private sector for development of tourism. State governments/district administration/local bodies, and councils are responsible for tourism at the regional and local level. The ministry sets out very specific rules and regulations for the hotel industry, which is entitled to various benefits including fiscal concessions and priority considerations for its various requirements. In Goa, planned tourism development started in 1965 but more concerted efforts began in 1982 with the setting up of the Goa Tourism Development Corporation. Other than this exercise and attempts to have tourism master plans in 1982 and again in 2001, the policy has been essentially a reactive one. In 2001, the government adopted a tourism policy for Goa. While this is more sensitive than earlier pronouncements to local concerns, it does not go far enough to address the concerns for a sustainable and quality coastal tourism.

Comments on the Policy

Several tensions, conflicts, and inconsistencies in policy are evident on the ground. Our comments here are two-fold.

1. Those that relate to coastal management policy more generally
2. Those that relate to coastal tourism more specifically.

Based on analysis of the policy, the following observations suggest possible reasons for the unsustainable use of coastal resources and negative impacts on the environment.

- The absence of a coastal focus in Indian policy results in little attention to the impacts of various sectoral polices on coastal resources use and on the need to connect development (in this case tourism) policy with environment policy. This is compounded by the approach to management of ocean resources and the environment at the national level and coastal development on the landward side at the state and local level, which results in redundant efforts, inefficiency, ineffectiveness, and lack of coordination among agencies.
- The human and social dimensions are missing in the coastal research policy in India. Most research and the institutions are of 'natural sciences'—heavy and focused on sciences and technology with no attention to the social aspects and the management of unsustainable human behaviour and consumption. There is little dialogue between these research communities, as a result integrated management and processes remain elusive. The end result is that a lot of the coastal research is not socially relevant and is unable to inform development issues.

- The wrong signals provided through liberal loans on concessional terms for setting up, deepening, and energizing water wells and subsidizing the supply of energy have been instrumental in increasing the rate and intensity of the depletion of groundwater. This has also prompted the growth of a water market in Goa, which meets the demand of the hotel industry that is, otherwise, unable to fulfill its needs from public water supply.
- No policy regime exists for groundwater use and quality control and no integrated conjunctive approach exists for the use of ground and surface water (Moench 1998a; 1998b).
- Regulations exist, but enforcement is poor or non-existent. The CRZ notification is violated in Goa and a number of other states as are Acts relating to water and air. Action constraining rules, such as source-specific standards, quotas on emissions and effluent discharges, land zoning, etc., are typical 'command-and control' mechanisms. This policy strategy, however, presupposes that the enforcement mechanisms, such as the administrative agencies and the judicial system, are in place and are able to act. If they do not, or cannot, for reasons of incapacity or political economy, the options available to individuals – though appearing to change – have, in fact, not changed, and the policy is ineffective in shaping environmental behaviour.

For the Industry

- Relatively high operating costs as compared to other destinations in Asia
- High taxation, both income tax and a multitude of sales and service taxes.

For the Tourist

- ❖ Lack of attention to visitor care
- ❖ Poor infrastructure
- ❖ Lack of cleanliness on the beach and surrounding areas
- ❖ Poor lighting and signage
- ❖ Time lags in obtaining visas and poor connectivity to Goa.

For the Host Population

- ❖ Lack of transparency of policy
- ❖ Insufficient attention to
- ❖ tourism multipliers income and employment
- ❖ Impacts on the environment, especially water availability social ills such pedophilia and HIV/AIDS.

Tourism can be transient, and overexposure can cause the tourist to move away, as has happened to many destinations of the world. Hence, a precautionary slant has to be adopted in policy to ensure that local communities are not affected badly in the event of such an occurrence.

Tourism can be a seductive activity, luring the youth with easy work and money. In the absence of attention to education and skill formation, there may be a loss of interest in such training other than that involves providing services to tourism such as singing, dancing, guiding, etc. In the event of tourism fading as an activity, we have a lost generation in terms of skills and readiness, as it cannot avail of the opportunities available in other markets.

Training to enhance the skills of the local people will not only infuse a greater professionalism in the services provided, but also empower the local communities and increase their maneuverability in terms of locations and occupations. There is need for policy to strengthen the local people as hosts.

Improving quality coastal tourist destinations is essential to satisfy tourists' needs, making the industry more competitive and ensuring that tourism develops in a balanced and sustainable way. Quality exists only to the extent that a product or a service meets the customer's requirements and expectations. Thus, in case of tourism, quality would mean taking into account and having a favourable impact on the activities of tourism professionals; tourists; the local population; and the environment, that is, the destination's natural, cultural, and manmade assets. Quality assessment should be based on the premises of visitor satisfaction; the satisfaction of tourism industry professionals; integration in the community, measured in terms of satisfaction of residents and other socio-economic agencies in the destination and its neighboring area; and environmental protection and sustainable use of natural and cultural resources (EC 2000).

The tourism industry, spoilt by success for a long time, seems to see only one way out of the crisis: more bargains. Big tour operators are able to largely pass on the pressure for increasingly lower prices to the holiday destinations. For in the negotiations, the destinations are bound to lose out to transnational corporations, which have – in the course of wide-ranging concentration processes in the industry during the past few years – often combined airlines and hotels, operating, marketing and sales in complex alliances under one roof and may switch to cheaper destinations at any time. Forcing down prices belongs to the wide range of unfair competitive practices in tourism. This has also been put down in writing by the UN Conference on Trade on Development, UNCTAD (Diaz Benavides 2001). According to an UNCTAD report, it is due to these "predatory practices" of tourism companies that poor countries earn too little from tourism and to financial leakages.

Sustainable Tourism

The concept of sustainability means that mankind must live within the capacity of the environment that supports. Sustainable development has been defined briefly as "that which meets the needs of the present without compromising the ability of future generations to meet their own needs".

The definition brings out certain important aspects of sustainable tourism:

- Conservation and enhancement of resources for the future generation
- Protection of biological diversity
- Equity within and between generations
- Integration of environmental, social and economic considerations

The concept of sustainable development is all about conservation and stewardship of resources for the future. The support for ecologically sustainable development emerging strongly in the tourism sector, as it is the logical way of balancing environmental concerns with growth and development of the industry. Environmental problems facing the world today are of such magnitude that urgent actions have to be taken at the highest levels to counter this fatal degradation. But it is not just enough for government organizations to work towards sustainable development. Every individual, every neighborhood, and every community has to contribute in every away possible to get close to the goal. Since the earth summit, the concept of sustainable development has been placed firmly on the global agenda. This issue is assuming great significance in the development of tourism in India also.

Tourism activities depend upon nature and natural heritage, it is essential to ensure that tourism development is ecologically sustainable –ecological process must not be neglected. Similarly tourism offers real experience of unique culture of the country. Hence the development should ensure that social and cultural sustainable tourism development compatible with the culture and values of the local people. The World Tourism Organization (WTO) defined sustainable tourism development as "that which meets the needs of present tourist and host regions while protecting and enhancing opportunities for the future. It is envisaged as leading to the management of all resources in such a way that economic, social and aesthetic needs can be fulfilled while maintaining cultural integrity, essential for ecological process, biological diversity and life supporting system".

Thus tourism has to be human and adapted to the needs of the tourist, respond to the needs of the local communities, be socio-economic and culturally well planned and environmentally sound. The tourism must offer products that are operated in harmony with the local environment, community attitudes and culture so that they become permanent beneficiaries and not the victims of tourism. The basic cultural identity of these local people should not be adversely affected. Sustainability also ensures economically sustainable-development process in the efficient management of resources and such management to ensure that the resource supports the future as well as the present generation.

Thus sustainable tourism aims to:

- ❖ Improve the quality of life of people.
- ❖ Provide good experience to the tourists
- ❖ Maintain the quality of environment that is essential for both tourists and the local community.

Tourism can be one of the effective tools for building a prosperous community economically, socially and culturally. It must be environmentally sustainable and based on the sustenance of the natural and cultural base. Each destination should examine whether it has adequate attractions and facilities for tourism and there is a potential for tourism generating markets to be open to exploitation. The carrying capacity is the central principle in environmental protection and sustainable tourism development. It determines the maximum use of any place without causing negative effects on resources on community, economy and culture. Thus tourism has to be environmentally sustainable in both natural and cultural environment.

Basic Guidelines for achieving sustainable tourism

The following are certain guidelines that have to be followed to achieve sustainable tourism:

- A general tourism policy incorporating sustainable tourism objectives at national regional and local level should be followed.
- Targets established for the planning, development and operation of tourism involving various government departments, public and private sector companies, community groups and experts could provide widest possible safeguards for success.
- Primary consideration should be given to the protection of natural and cultural assets.
- All tourism participants will follow ethical and sound behavioral and conservative rules regarding nature, culture, economy, and community value system.
- The distribution of tourism development project should be rationed on the basis of equity.
- Public awareness of benefits tourism and how to mitigate its negative impacts should be pursued.

- ❖ Local people would be encouraged to assume leadership roles in planning and development.

In the Tourism Policy, 1982 the guidelines in Eco-tourism have attempted to achieve sustainability in tourism. It indicates that the key players in the ecotourism are Central Government and state governments, local authorities, developers, operators, visitors and local community. Each of them has to be sensitive to the environment and local traditions and follow the guidelines for successfully development of sustainable tourism. "Policy guidelines state that tourism must contribute to the better understanding between different cultures and to economic development. In reality we find that tourism is neither a tool for cultural exchange nor is it an ideal model for economic development. It has been observed in several countries like Philippines, Thailand and Srilanka that the unchecked or unquestioned growth of tourism can't escape from exploiting people. The problems are there to be seen. It has taken a long time for NGOs and other interest groups to point out the negative impacts of modern tourism and bring them into focus. It has taken an equally long time for these groups to make the Tourism industry acknowledge it's impacts. It is the product of this relentless pressure on the tourism industry that the National Associations of Travel Agents and Tour Operators within the European Union castigated any form of sexual exploitation of children and pledged never to promote tours with pedophile purposes.

The national tourism policy, which was approved by the Cabinet recently, attempts to position the sector as a major engine of economic growth and harness its direct and multiplier effects for employment generation, economic development and to provide impetus to rural tourism. In a statement in the Lok Sabha, the Union Tourism Minister, Mrs Ambika Soni, said that the policy attempted to position India as a global brand to take advantage of the burgeoning global travel and the vast untapped potential of the country as a destination. Besides, the policy sought to acknowledge the critical role of the private sector, with the Government working as a pro-active facilitator and catalyst. The Minister added that the policy was based on the principle that in the four decades or so, a tourism revolution has been sweeping the world with the number of tourists leaving their homes worldwide increasing from 100 million during 1964 to 700 million during 2001 and likely to swell to 1.5 billion by 2020 with receipts estimated to cross $2,000 billion. "If India has to partake in this revolution in a meaningful way, it must change its strategies as well as the techniques and tools of its machinery of implementation. In this connection, it has to be noted with concern that during the last decade or so, India's share of world tourist traffic has remained static at 0.38 per cent," Mrs. Ambika Soni said.

At the institutional level, a framework would have to be evolved, which is Government-led, private sector-driven and community welfare-oriented. The Minister also dwelt on the fact that effective linkages and close coordination should be established with the departments of civil aviation, environment, forest, railway and home, among others. Further, he said that sustainability should serve as a guiding star for the new policy and added that the development and management strategies should be so worked out as to ensure that tourism largely acted as a smokeless industry and its ecological footprints remained as soft as possible. "No one engaged, directly or indirectly, in the tourism industry, should be allowed to secure short-term gains by resorting to what has been called the darker side of tourism," the Minister said.

Besides, the tourist industry and travel agents should be persuaded to "evolve and adopt" voluntarily a code of ethics and its infringement should be firmly dealt with by the tours and travel association, he added. At the international level, the country should play a dynamic role and make its presence felt at the world tourism organization, world tourism and travel council and earth council.

POLICY OF DELHI GOVERMENT

The Tourism Department is responsible for promotion of domestic and international tourism, development of tourism related infrastructure, licensing of tour operators/ travel agents. It is also entrusted with the supervision of two agencies: Delhi Tourism and Transportation Development Corporation (DTTDC) and Delhi Institute of Hotel Management and Catering Technology (DIHMCT).

The Department has the following responsibilities:

1. Promotion of domestic and international tourism
2. Development of tourism related infrastructure
3. Coordination with agencies involved in tourism industry
4. Classification of hotels
5. Licensing of tour operators, travel agents
6. Delhi Tourism and Transportation Development Corporation (DTTDC)
7. Delhi Institute of Hotel Management and Catering Technology (DIHMCT)

Reforms

- ❖ The Department of Tourism should not be in the business of selling liquor. This should be left to private players.
- ❖ When the government does not have money to provide drinking water, it should not venture into

running a hotel management institute. Such vocational education can be safely left to the private sector.

- ❖ Festivals and fairs should be organized by trade and community associations.
- ❖ The activities of the Department are largely a form of corporate welfare: taxpayers' money is used to subsidies businesses. The 'profit' earned by selling liquor is also ultimately taxpayers' money.

The Government has tightened the import regime for motor cars, sports utility vehicles (SUVs) and all-purpose vehicles under the export promotion capital goods (EPCG) scheme by hotels, travel and tourism and golf tourism sectors. The move comes in the wake of misuse of the EPCG scheme for import of cars by some segments of the travel and tourism industry. The Directorate-General of Foreign Trade (DGFT) has now stipulated that import of motor cars, SUVs and all-purpose vehicles under the EPCG scheme would be allowed only to hotels, travel agents, tour operators or tour transport operators and companies owning or operating golf resorts whose total foreign exchange earning from these specific businesses in the current and preceding three licensing years is Rs 1.5 crore or more. Moreover, the Government said the 'duty saved' amount on all EPCG licenses issued in a licensing year from import of motor cars, SUVs and all-purpose vehicles should not exceed 50 per cent of the average foreign exchange earnings from the hotel, travel and tourism and golf tourism sectors in the preceding three licensing years. Commenting on the Government's move to bring in new conditions on car imports under the EPCG scheme by the hotel, travel and tourism sector, Mr Ajai Sahai, Director-General, Federation of Indian Export Organizations (FIEO), told Business Line that these steps would curb the misuse of the EPCG scheme. Delhi

Government has decided that 20 per cent of around 6,000 modern, low-floor buses — to hit the capital's roads before the Commonwealth Games to be held in 2010 — will be air conditioned.

CONSUMER PROTECTION

Consumer protection is a form of government regulation which protects the interests of consumers. For example, a government may require businesses to disclose detailed information about products—particularly in areas where safety or public health is an issue, such as food. Consumer protection is linked to the idea of consumer rights (that consumers have various rights as consumers), and to the formation of consumer organizations which help consumers make better choices in the marketplace. Consumer interests can also be protected by promoting competition in the markets which directly and indirectly serve consumers, consistent with economic efficiency, but this topic is treated in Competition law. Consumer protection law or consumer law is considered an area of public law that regulates private law relationships between individual consumers and the businesses that sell those goods and services. Consumer protection covers a wide range of topics, including but not necessarily limited to product liability, privacy rights, unfair business practices, fraud, misrepresentation, and other consumer/business interactions. Such laws deal with credit repair, debt repair, product safety, service contracts, bill collector regulation, pricing, utility turnoffs, consolidation, personal loans that may lead to bankruptcy and much more.

The tourism industry, spoilt by success for a long time, seems to see only one way out of the crisis: more bargains. Big tour operators are able to largely pass on the pressure for increasingly lower prices to the holiday destinations. For in the negotiations, the destinations are bound to lose out to transnational corporations, which have – in the course of wide-ranging concentration processes in the industry during the past few years – often combined airlines and hotels, operating, marketing and sales in complex alliances less than one roof and may switch to cheaper destinations at any time. Forcing down prices belongs to the wide range of unfair competitive practices in tourism. This has also been put down in writing by the UN Conference on Trade on Development, UNCTAD (Diaz Benavides 2001). According to an UNCTAD report, it is due to these "predatory practices" of tourism companies that poor countries earn too little from tourism and to financial leakages, for example, for tourism-related imports. UNCTAD concludes that in certain cases, poor destinations even subsidies rich tourists. In order to survive in the face of global competition, many destinations offer generous conditions to foreign investors and companies, such as tax relief, majority holdings in companies or free repatriation of profits. These investment incentives are usually granted in the context of measures against indebtedness, recommended by creditors and by the International Monetary Fund (IMF) in order to generate foreign exchange by promoting tourism. All in all, however, this means a considerable loss of income for the public treasury, while the provision of expensive infrastructure such as airports, roads, water and energy supplies for tourism often continues to increase the debt burden. Since the mid- 1990s, liberalization to the advantage of foreign private companies has been continuously expanded. Under the General Agreement on Trade in Services (GATS) of the World Trade Organization (WTO-OMC), import barriers have been reduced and employing foreign personnel has become easier. The GATS is currently being re-negotiated. This has led to strong controversies in the member countries about the future of public services such as water supply or education. But the new round of negotiations also raises serious concerns on the side of non-governmental organizations (NGOs) in the South as well as in the North with regard to the future development of tourism. The Indian tourism NGO Equations, for example, criticizes that the service agreement on tourism undermines national regulations and local self-government, and poses a threat to the livelihoods of people in the tourism destinations. Once the agreements have been concluded, it is almost impossible to insist on the obligation of foreign suppliers to train and employ local personnel, or to maintain social and ecological standards, to ensure consumer protection or to enforce restrictions, such as limitations to the number or size of golf courses or hotels and resorts in protected areas (Equations 2002, 2003).

Approaches to fair trade in tourism

Clearly, Fair Trade offers perspectives for the urgently needed new orientation in tourism. Demands for fair trade structures and a fair distribution of profits move socioeconomic and political concerns to the centre of attention – the so-called „social dimension", which had so far been largely neglected in the strive for sustainability in tourism. This has also been admitted by tourism leaders on the occasion of the World Summit on Sustainable Development last year in Johannesburg (WTO 2002). Furthermore, in order to achieve Fair Trade, the various actors along the supply chain – producers and consumers, wholesalers, manufacturer and retailers – all have to become simultaneously active and make their respective contribution. This framework of action goes far beyond the selective approaches of previous efforts towards sustainable tourism.

Skeptics might argue that in the current tourism crisis it is a hopeless venture to involve the various actors in measures that actually bring about Fair Trade in Tourism. The crisis, however, is - due to bomb attacks, kidnappings and wars – also an expression of the increasing insecurity of tourists. It is exactly this crisis, which encourages (or forces) actors in tourism to search for new, socially responsible approaches. The interest in Fair Trade in Tourism is growing. NGOs in the North and in the South that have always been the driving forces in Fair Trade, have already prepared the ground well and have at various levels of action laid promising foundations. These approaches are now to be linked, and consistent campaigning and advocacy must push for the implementation of Fair Trade in Tourism.

Thanks to the Fair Trade in Tourism project of Tourism Concern, tourism initiatives and NGOs from all continents were able to develop - sometimes in heated discussions - common criteria for Fair Trade in Tourism. They have continued to refine these criteria in their daily work. One result is the certification process of FTTSA in South Africa, where a new label for individual tourism products has set new quality standards. This label has – unlike most other labels in tourism – been developed by the people actually concerned. It rings in a paradigm shift in tourism: the needs of local communities for (existential) security and quality (of life) rate at least as high as the demands of the tourists for quality and security which had so far been the only deciding factor in the design of tourism projects (even though the so called needs of the tourists often corresponded to the needs of market research institutes and their weighty clients in the tourism industry). For such products, a clear, credible label on social responsibility can become an important marketing instrument. Many innovative tourism projects are currently making efforts to give local communities a fairer share in tourism in the South as well as in the North. All these projects will eventually need to get market access (see box "Something out of Nothing"). Many of these service providers bet on international tourism right from the outset.

For years, business leaders have been recommending tourism as a promising path to development. Recently, it has also been increasingly promoted as a tried and tested instrument of "poverty alleviation". These new initiatives, however, hardly find their way into the catalogues of tour operators, nor do they get access to global reservation systems where distribution channels, particularly in international tourism, converge. Every project is invariably faced with the question of how much effort is involved in getting access to the international market, and how much dependency will result from trying to survive in a highly competitive globalised environment. Proven development experts have been justified in pointing out to the Fair Trade movement time and again that market access alone does not automatically result in Fair Trade (Bello 2002). Trading partners are needed and also specific support, which goes beyond mere trade aspects. This may include targeted development co-operation Development agencies have recently started to increasingly turn to tourism. However, they often invest in tourism projects without adequately taking into account the global context of an economic sector, which is highly interlinked. They have also not first focused on the empowerment of communities in the tourism destinations. This, however, would be necessary for local people to obtain the right qualifications to deal with new challenges and to above all be able to protect their rights, including their participation in decision-making processes, a share in the benefits, protection against exploitation and access to the resources which secure their livelihoods, but which are at the same time important „inputs"for tourism. The "empowerment" of local communities is also the key to a fair exchange between hosts and guests.

At the same time, tourists, who travel to the service providers and "consume" services in the destination itself, are an integral part of trade. Once they have made their booking, they must know clearly how they can contribute to Fair Trade during their holiday. For example, a fair exchange with the hosts includes respecting the limitations they may set to their own hospitality. Or, a fair price does not only have to cover the full costs of resource consumption, but also the service of protecting biological diversity and safeguarding local cultures and traditions. NGOs in countries where tourists are from are required to provide sound background information and to develop new instruments to raise tourist awareness. They carry out broad-based consumer campaigns, presenting tangible options that go far beyond the tips for adequate behavior that tourists have been presented with for years.

Ethical Tourism in the Context of Consumer Protection

Ethical tourism will rightly be a big issue in the new millennium. The experience of working with international partners in the developing world indicates the need for it. As the public have more free time available and more money to spend on leisure (in the last 30 years the average spending on leisure has almost doubled from 9% to 17% of household income), and as an increasing number of people travel to developing countries, they will want to ensure that their holiday will help, and not hinder, development. Although some parts of the industry have responded to environmental concerns, there has been a worrying lack of activity to improve the wider impact of tourism on local people. With increasing competition in the industry, the companies that dare to become more ethical and respond to this unmet consumer demand will be able to gain a competitive edge.

Choosing a holiday

Unsurprisingly the three main criteria are weather, cost and good facilities. But tourists do show concern about ethical policies and environmental considerations. Surprisingly, there is little brand loyalty: the bottom-scoring criterion for choosing a holiday was having used the company before; this suggests tour companies need to respond carefully to consumer demands.

Holiday information and behaviour

The public want to behave in an appropriate manner when overseas and be responsible travellers. They are keen to fit in with the local customs and want to ensure that their holidays support the local economy. They are particularly interested in receiving information on 'local customs and appropriate dress and behaviour' and on 'ways to support the local economy and meet the local people'. Contrary to some beliefs, most tourists do not simply want to live in a 'sanitized bubble' whilst on holiday.

Information - whose responsibility?

Most think that tour operators and travel agents have the prime responsibility to provide the information they require on a wide range of issues - both before they go on holiday and once they are there. The tourism industry would therefore do well to respond to these consumer demands for more information so that the tourists themselves and those in the host destination get the most out of the holiday.

The price of principles

Over half would be willing to pay more for their overseas holiday if they were guaranteed that the 'money goes towards preservation of the local environment, workers in the destinations are guaranteed good wages and working conditions, or money goes to support a local charity'.

Tour companies take note

Nearly half of those questioned said they would be more likely to go with a 'company that had a written code to guarantee good working conditions, protect the environment and support local charities in the tourist destination'. Taken with the fact that there is low brand loyalty, this willingness to go with more ethical companies is both a warning and a positive opportunity to companies who are expecting to lead the way in the Indian tourism industry at the start of the new millennium: 'Change in line with changing public attitudes or be left behind!'

In the footsteps of fair-trade

The research also tested the assumption that there are particular groups who will be more aware of the ethical issues involved in tourism. The assumption proved founded: the highest scoring groups were those who 'regularly buy fair trade or use an ethical bank or investment fund', are 'members of an environmental, development or human rights group' or 'have been on a trip to a developing country, or plan to do so in the next few years.' This shows that, in an increasingly globalised world, people are beginning to make the connections between their actions as consumers and the effects on the producers, and to change their behaviour. The massive growth of the fair-trade movement in the 1990s demonstrates that many are willing to positively choose, and pay a premium for, the products of companies which guarantee good working conditions and fair wages to their producers.

Security and economic concerns are still significant factors affecting travel decisions; globally and across demographic sectors. Continued currency value realignment (particularly the reduced value of the US dollar against the Euro) will continue to shape consumer and industry spending decisions. Tourists, overall, are not curtailing their travel, so much as spending less (tourism receipts have decreased more than have the number of international arrivals), and staying closer to home. This has led to an increase in regional and local tourism. Regional budget airline growth is also fueling this trend (The continued viability of their business models remains to be seen, however).

Major new outbound markets are developing in China, India, Russia and other ex-Soviet countries, and to a lesser extent, the Middle East, as a result of economic and social changes in these countries. The Asian markets among these are tending to produce mostly regional travel demand, which should help Asian tourism rebound from losses in previous years. New pressures and new roles. The global security and economic situation remains volatile, and rapid technological innovation looks to remain the norm. Wider availability of new communications technologies will change tourism markets in ways we have not yet imagined. Flexibility, diversification, and decentralization seem certain to become more important for the survival and success of tourism organizations and tourism-based economies.

Internet travel purchases (now the largest amount of all online purchases) and airline competition have led to a downward pressure on prices and slimmer profit margins for tour operators, travel agents, and throughout much of the industry; in general, leading to necessary realignments within the industry.

More competing tourism products, decreased customer loyalty, and increases in last-minute booking present challenges to tourism organizations. They will need to work harder to differentiate their products and services, help tourists sort through the "information clutter", engender trust and loyalty, and maintain stable revenue flows. Smart marketers appear capable of countering the above trends and displacing price's centrality in purchase decisions for some types of travel products. More sophisticated uses of these new communication technologies, such as Internet-enabled customer relationship management tools and email marketing campaigns, would allow for more selective marketing and distribution strategies to attract highly desirable tourists. Internet and other new communications tools are displacing some tourism intermediaries and redefining the roles of others. Tourism product suppliers are less reliant on traditional distribution intermediaries, and consumers are more willing to make their own travel arrangements. The WTO notes that the current emphasis on regional travel is also producing less group travel and more individual travel (people feel more confident to make their own arrangements, when the destinations are more familiar).

Trust is more than ever a central concern for travel purchasers. By nature, the product cannot be tried before purchase, and businesses on the Web must still overcome a healthy skepticism about the trustworthiness of the companies and offers they discover online. Speedy decision-making is also important, as the most frequent travelers are often also the most pressed for time; particularly as the number of competing tourism choices threatens to overwhelm their ability to choose. There is an important opportunity for "experts" to support decision-making about tourism purchases. Agents and intermediaries which add real value with their specialist expertise and personal service will remain relevant and successfully navigate the shifting roles in travel distribution.

New demand and opportunities for sustainable tourism. Even the smallest operators, like community-based tourism groups, can generate their own demand. Where distributors remain necessary, they can negotiate distribution from a position of greater strength, and reduce price pressure on their tourism products.

While price pressures and competition have characterized most parts of the industry, there has been sustained or increased demand for luxury accommodations, tours, and other travel packages. The trends are not mutually exclusive within one set of purchase decisions: "Luxury travelers" may choose budget transportation, expensive accommodations, and adventure tours (which might previously have been seen as incongruous choices). More consumer access to information, better product customization, and more attention to demand-led marketing are both revealing and producing more complex travel purchase habits. The "package holiday" approach to tourism products may be on its way out. An increase (2-3% from 1993-2003) in tour customizations may be related to this trend toward individualization. Active travelers have not been deterred by security concerns, but have also traveled more regionally. Self-identified "active travelers" intend to increase travel expenditures over the next few years. According to the World Tourism Organization, "active travelers" rate available activities higher than destination in terms of importance to their purchase decisions.

Eco-tourism, nature tourism, hard adventure, soft adventure, sports tourism, and health tourism count among the top growth sectors. For example, the World Tourism Organization estimates that the market for nature tourism is increasing at 6 times the rate of tourism overall. There appears to be evidence for a "self-actualization" dividend (if not a "green dividend") for tourism sales. There are signs of increasing interest in travel for reasons of personal growth, assertion of individuality, human connection, and "authentic experience", among segments of major outbound markets. These segments overlap markets for "luxury experience" and new, "exotic", "individual" consumer goods. These travelers appear more flexible about price

("price elastic"), when they can be convinced that an experience offers significant additional value (in terms of the interests listed above).

These consumer and lifestyle groups have been called "Cultural Creative's" in the USA; "New Authentic", "Style-Lifers" and "Neo-consumers" in Europe (the groups and findings represented by these terms are not totally interchangeable, but appear to overlap more than not on characteristics important to tourism decisions). As an example of these groups' significance: the original research done about "Cultural Creative's" showed they represent 25% of the adult U.S. population at the time of the study—the polling group American Lives estimates that they amount to 50 million people including both the U.S.A. and Europe. The desirability of market segments which use travel consciously as a means of personal growth and a defining "lifestyle accessory" will lead to increased use of "lifestyle marketing" through partnerships with producers of psychologically-associated products and related organizations. These tourists require different marketing approaches; they appear not to respond well to direct marketing, for example; are avid media consumers; and tend to require corroboration of information from a trusted authority or personal acquaintance.

Sustainable tourism products are poised to take advantage of the preceding trends, as lifestyle products in line with the demand for organic foods, Fair Trade products, and "natural health-care", all "luxury," "individual", and "authentic" products, of demonstrated appeal to people in these "new lifestyle" groups. Sustainability is of increasing concern to tourism organizations of all sectors. The effort at "greening" tourism is now the focus of hundreds of initiatives and conferences, as well as certification efforts, worldwide. Many of the largest institutional donors have recognized its validity and value as an approach and a goal, and include sustainability as a central criterion in their development packages—and major donors are increasingly turning to tourism development to achieve overall development goals.

Tourism is not just an economic transaction or a series of activities which can be isolated from everyday life or from their impact on people. The very fact that tourism involves travel to another culture and direct contact with the people there, raises a number of ethical issues. Do local people want tourists visiting them? What are the working conditions in the tourism industry? What change does tourism make to local relationships and values? Where does the money go - who benefits? What are the environmental consequences of travel? Does travelling to a particular place support democracy and human rights, or undermine them? Tourism to developing countries is growing and has a disproportionate impact on the poor. They may gain access to the jobs in the industry and receive new opportunities to provide goods and services. However, they also live in the (often rural) areas which receive the most destructive forms of tourism, thus bearing the brunt without reaping the benefits. The poor suffer the worst effects and they should be the focus of any improvements. Tourism is not just an economic issue but also a social one as there are numerous contingent relationships established between the buyer and those involved in the production, manufacture, marketing and selling. Tourism is one of the global industries which have the greatest impact on people and it should therefore have their well-being, especially those on the receiving end, as its foundation. The people who live on the land, open up their homes and their lives, and provide services for tourists are those whose concerns should be first.

Responsible Tourim Guidelines

As members of AITO we recognise that in carrying out our work as tour operators we have a responsibility to respect other people's places and ways of life. We acknowledge that wherever a tour operator does business or sends clients it has a potential to do both good and harm, and we are aware that all too often in the past the harm has outweighed the good.

All tourism potentially has an environmental, social and economic impact on the destination involved. We accept, therefore, that we as tour operators should aim to be responsible in all our dealings on each of these three levels. To help us to do so we have proposed a set of guidelines intended to help companies, customers and local suppliers recognise their common responsibilities to:

- protect the environment - its flora, fauna and landscaps.
- respect local cultures - traditions, religions and built heritage
- benefit local communities - both economically and socially
- conserve natural resources - from office to destination
- minimise pollution - though noise, waste, disposal and congestion.

We are an association of individual, independent companies, each with our own distinctive style and field of operation. As uch, we each have our own ways of fulfilling the details of these responsibilities by:

- establishing our own policies and involving our staff,
- informing our clients about responsible tourism and, where appropriate,
- encouraging them to participate
- working with our suppliers and partners to achieve responsible goals and practices
- publicising good practice to encourage and spread responsible tourism.

If India is to realize its enormous potential in tourism it must provide exclusive world-class tourism products and destinations to compete successfully for a larger share of the Asian tourism market. Today, outbound tourism from India far exceeds visitor traffic to the country partly because there is a lack of world-class destinations within the country and partly because the domestic tourism policy has been largely directed towards those in the lower end of the spending spectrum. The high spender from India prefers to visit neighboring countries as he gets better value for money. The scope and reach of domestic tourism will have to be broadened in the next plan through the development of competitive destinations that match international standards in terms of price and quality and also satisfy the international traveller. India's international arrival figures have not been able to keep pace with neighboring countries and have been exceeded by Thailand, Malaysia, Indonesia, Dubai and the Maldives. Since 1995, India's share of the world market has remained virtually stagnant at 0.38 per cent, while domestic tourism has grown at a phenomenal rate and India now accounts for 4.6 per cent share of domestic tourism worldwide. In terms of tourism receipts, India has shown relative buoyancy because of the interest shown by visitors in traditional handicraft items and particularly in diamonds. The Next

Plan visualizes a mutually supportive role for tourism and handicrafts by encouraging Haats and Shilpgrams and recognizing shopping as an integral part of the tourism experience to promote the 'Made in India' brand.

Consumer Protection Act, 1986

Codes of conduct or of ethics are a mechanism to regulate the impact of tourism and maintain tourist satisfaction. Much of tourism's impact results from the activities of inexperienced visitors. Besides knowing there are established legal regulations backed by enforcement, visitors to protected areas need and usually appreciate guidelines and information on how to behave. Codes of conduct should also target tour operators. Legal enforcement of regulations will be less necessary if management of the protected area effectively inform, persuade, and educate their tour operators about codes of conduct and ask for their cooperation. Awareness and well advertised codes of conduct for both visitors and tour operators are key to the success of this strategic policy option in preventing unnecessary tourism impact.

4

Impact of promotional activities on Tourism in New Delhi

Marketing Mix

Tourist marketing mix is largely a complex group of Factors intervening to achieve the marketing end product which is increased effectiveness in demand output in relation to supply and marketing investment by tourist enterprises.

The term marketing mix introduced by Professor NEIL Broders in 1953 when he got the clue from a study of management of marketing costs, which described the marketing executive as a mixture of ingredients.

Philip Kotler has defined the marketing mix as, 'The set of marketing tools that the firm uses to pursue its marketing objectives in the target market." Generally the Marketing Mix constitutes the four P's i.e., product, price, promotion and place.

Besides these 4Ps in a service industry like tourism, another fifth (People, process and Physical evidence) is also much relevance. Each sector tourism industry has its own requirements in terms of designing the product. At the same time in the tourism marketing mix one must also take note of the attitudes and aspirations of the host populations.

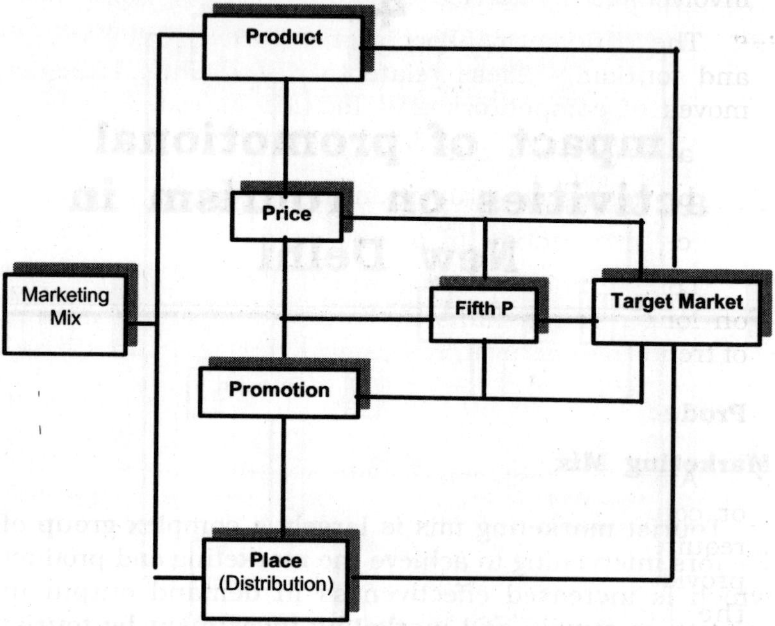

There are several challenges in case of tourism products because of its different features like intangibility, perish ability, inseparability, heterogeneous and seasonally. Service manager or tour operator faces challenges of tourism products are consistency in quality, managing customers, missing inventory intangibility of offer and absence of patent protection necessitate still that are not possessed by goods manager. The activities in tourism marketing are different and do not fall in the conventional Marketing Mix classification, though many marketing connects and tools used by goods marketer hold good in services with some change in focus and importance. Therefore conventional marketing mix needs to be modified and broadened so keeping in mind these challenges fifth is prescribed which is consists of people, process and physical evidence these are essential to meet the challenge posed by intangibility, service provider, customer interaction and customer involvement in service consumption and production.

The short-term aspects of marketing mix in travel and tourism – these relate to meeting the immediate moves of competitors and include aspects like.

a. Price reduction; hotels

b. Aggressive promotion; charters

c. Introduction of a new product.

Long term aspects of marketing mix – these are based on longer range plans derived from study of all kinds of trends like natural, economic, social and technological.

Product

Anything that can be offered in a market for use or consumption by the consumers as per the market requirement is called product. For example a beach resort provides, sun, sea relaxation and entertainment. Hence, the beach resort is a tourism product for the consumption and use of tourists. According to Philip Kotler "A product is anything that can be offered to a market for attention, acquisition, use or consumption that might satisfy a want or need".

There are certain factors associated with a product and these include: basic design, presentation, quality, range, brand, image, image, warranties, customer protection & eco friendly etc.

Medlik and Middleton have observed that "As far as the tourist is concerned the product covers the complete experience from the time he leaves home to the time he returns to it." Designing the product is the base on which all other aspects of the Marketing Mix will be constructed. Product in tourism is certainly different from consumer goods like biscuit, soap, drinks, etc. In tourism it is basically the services like transport, accommodation, facilities at destination etc., that you package as a product along with attractions. Because of this specific nature of tourism product it is essential to understand the factors that influence the formulation of product in tourism. Identification of the market segment and its requirements is the first step in devising the product. Quality and service to be offered to the customers play a decisive role in the success of a product. In the formulation of a product it is necessary to consider that customers buy products for the benefits they deliver. Another important aspects is matching supply to demand and is that the product or service is tied up or linked with a chain of products over which one has not any control. This calls for thinking about and having the right type of linkage to overcome the problems of inter-dependence at the product design stage itself. There are situations when two or more organizations go for joint product design ventures.

DEFINATION

Anything that can be offered in a market for use, consumption by the consumers as per the market requirement is called product. For example a beach resort provides sun, sea ,relaxation and entertainment. Hence a beach resort is a tourism product. According to Philip Kotler "A product is anything that can be offered in the market for attention ,acquisition, use or consumption that might satisfy a want or need." He has mentioned five product levels that marketer should in to consideration for development of any product.

Level 1 Core benefit This is the fundamental service or benefit being bought by the customer.

Level 2 Generic product When the marketer converts the core benefit into a basic version of the product it is termed as generic product.

Level 3 Expected products The customers generally expect a set of attributes and conditions while making a purchase and if the marketer meets the expectations it is termed as expected product.

Level 4 Augmented products When a product is developed with such additional services or benefits which make it distinctive from other products it is termed as an augmented product.

Level 5 Potential product This indicates the possible evolution if the augmented product. This where organizations search for new ideas and at same time make their product unique or different. To explain these levels through the example of a service product. Food is a core benefit which is being bought by customer. A restaurant converts food with its brand name There is in a restaurant good food, service, staff and kitchen are the generic benefits. Cleanliness timely service ,polite and courteous behavior, menu availability and music are expected benefits. Sparking floors, smiling employees courtesy welcome note and music of choice are augmented product and restaurant manager by adding extra dish with some food could make it different product. Potential product which is beyond the usual like manager's words of thanks.

By using these five levels a marketer can make a product different product From the competition it helps to gain more customers and lead to brand loyalty. Besides these certain factors associated with a product these include:

- ❖ **Basic design,** i.e. the size or say the quantity and level of services.
- ❖ **Presentation ,i.e.** the environment and atmosphere in which the service is being provided.

- **Quality, i.e.** the standard of service to be offered and maintained – something very important in tourism.
- **Range, i.e.** what all is to be included in the product or covered in the service.
- **Brand, i.e**. association of a name, which is well known or associated, with high levels of customer satisfaction.
- **Image, i. e.** a reputation earned by the product.
- **Warranties, i.e.** an assurance of a particular level and quality of service.
- **Consumer protection, i.e.** assurance of damage's claim in the environment conservation
- **Eco friendly, i.e.** care for ecology and environment.

In travel and tourism product may defined as a package of a various components. These components are:

- Destination attractions.
- Destination facilities and services.
- Accessibility of the destination.
- Experiences at the destination.
- Attitudes of locale or host population.
- Price to the consumer.

To understand the product from the standpoint of the tourist, Medlick and middleton have observed that "as far as the tourist product is concerned the products covers the complete experience from the time he leaves to the time he returns to it". Let it explain it further, suppose a family plans to visit Manali. In this particular case various services needed by the said family like transport, accommodation, facilities and services at the destination. A tour operator can package all these services or family can approach to different functionaries for particular services. So what is important to analyze all the possible requirements of a tourist during the course of a visit to a destination. In the case cited, the entire experience right from leaving Delhi to coming back home is the product. Middelton has noted that researching targeted customer's perceptions of product benefits and utilities, and designing or adopting to match their expectations, lies if course at the heart of marketing theory. Segmenting the target market and then understandings customers preferences and motivations, which constantly change, is the to product formulation.

DEVELOPING A PRODUCT

Products are developed primarily to satisfy the customer's needs. While developing a product a marketer must go through a process. Fist step in the development of a product is to collect information about the market requirement. It can be done through market research.

Business analysis is second step, this is to be used to eliminate poor ideas which occurred while going through the process of market research. Business analysis is a process of estimating future sales and profit of a new product. Besides this economic aspect, other aspects of the product i.e. promotion, distribution and image must not be ignored.

A kind of test run of the product is done before launching the because chances of failures always remain in any product. Final stage in the development of a product is commercialization, which refers to full-scale production and distribution of a product it must be remembered that designing a product is base on which all other aspects of Marketing Mix will be constructed.

PRODUCT MIX

It Here

- Is also necessary to be familiar with the concept of Product Mix. Philip Kotler has mentioned that "Product Mix is a set of all products within a product mix that a particular organization makes available to customers." He has further defined Product line and Product item.
- Product line is a group of products within a product mix that are closely related, either because they function in a similar manner, are made available to the same consumers, or marketed through the same type outlets.
- Product item is a distinct unit with a product line that is distinguishable by size, appearance, price or some other attribute.

DEVISING PRODUCT IN TOURISM

Product in tourism is certainly different from consumer's goods like soap, drinks etc. In tourism it is basically the services like transport, accommodation, facilities at destination, etc. that one can package as a product along with attractions. Because of this specific nature of tourism it is essential to understand the factors that a formulation of product in tourism.

Identification of market segment and its requirements is the first step in devising the product Suppose one wants to start tour operator business and there are already a lot of tour operators in market .But through market analysis one reach a conclusions that there is a market for adventure tours. Accordingly one plans to offer packages in adventure tourism.

Quality and service to be offered to the customers play a decisive role in the success of a product Quality involves a kind of assurance on the standard of product. Particularly in tourism sector it is important to create a reputation for the good quality of the product and service offered. It provides a better credibility of your company in the market. In tourism where the perception of risk is a very high among tourists, a company assures higher quality service it is bound to be successful.

In the formulation of a product it is necessary to consider that customers buy products for the benefits they deliver. It is therefore important to add certain features in your product, which will to differentiate it from competitors. However, in providing special facilities or advantages business norms and ethics to be maintained.

Another important aspect is matching the supply to demand. So far as demand is concerned the marketing manager should gather information about customer's needs, behavior and perceptions in order to define target segments to identify the strength and weakness of existing products. So far supply is concerned the marketing managers task involves analyzing product components and identifying the range of existing and potential products which would be improved or developed. profitably to meet customer's needs. Ideally there should be combination of products which are well established in the market and new products as per demand of the prevailing market.

Michael M Contemn has mentioned three types of orientation for product design in tourism.

1) **Product Orientation:** This lay stress on the products and services of tourism supply rather taking into account the tourists requirements. The success of this approach can be if the demand exceeds supply or in a monopoly situation.

2) **Market Orientation:** This approach emphasis on the requirement of the target market segments. However, this approach ignores the local population and local natural resources, customs and culture etc. and runs the risk of not only alienating the host population but generating anti – tourism feelings.

3) **Societal Orientation:** This in fact is an approach which balances the market oriented approach with the interests of the host population and attempts to minimize the negative impacts on the society, environment, culture, etc.

Societal Orientation is a must in tourism. Generally tourism organizations ignore it while designing and marketing their products. This appears to be beneficial but in fact the benefits will be always short lived.

There are certain factors that need attention, while designing or packaging tourism products.

- ❖ Carrying capacity of the destination,
- ❖ Safety and security,
- ❖ Hygienic conditions,
- ❖ Attitude of host population,
- ❖ Government rules and regulations,
- ❖ Environment preservation and conservation,
- ❖ Linkages with local bodies and host population.

In fact all these aspects have a bearing on the experience for the tourists and help in doing away weak link with the product line. The challenge before the tourism marketer is to transform routine into a unique experience and this needs creativity as well as imagination.

Seasonally besides other features is a important feature which needs proper handling in relation to marketing and designing the product. The highly elastic tourism is to a large extent linked with seasonally aspect. Both the tourist generating markets as well as destinations have seasonal limitations. There are peak seasons and lean seasons, which are measured in terms of the demand and supply situation. An analysis tourist's arrival at any destinations would demonstrate monthly fluctuations. For example there may be more rush in summer at any hill station in comparison to winter. Such analysis is extremely useful from the point of view as it helps in deciding the marketing mix. For example, products can be designed, rejuvenated, or dropped as per the seasonal requirements. Similarly, separate price may be charged for lean seasons along with a different promotion policy. So by careful planning or devising marketer can meet the challenge of seasonality of tourism product.

PRODUCT POSITIONING

Tourism destinations or tourism products and services have an image or perception in the customer's mind, which is built over the years. For example many countries or destinations have been struggling hard to improve their image in the tourist generating markets inspire of having good tourism products like India that has different destinations to visit but because of poverty, infrastructure constrains like transport network and accommodation facilities. Before we discuss further it must be noted here that an understanding of market segments or designing products for the targeted segment alone is not enough. There are many offering similar products, which satisfy tourists needs. Under these circumstances it is the uniqueness and quality of your products that determine the image and identity. Hence we ought to be familiarize with the concepts of differentiation's and positioning. According to Kotler –

- ❖ Differentiation is the act of designing a set of meaningful differences to distinguish the company's offer from competitors' offers.
- ❖ Positioning is the act of designing the company's offer and image so that it occupies distinct and valued place in the target customer' minds.

In tourism it is not just company but the country or the destinations, which too has to adopt differentiation and positioning in the international as well as domestic markets. One has to take decision regarding how many differences to promote in comparison to one's competitors. However, these decisions should be taken after keeping in view the various products in the market, their attributes and image etc. however, product should not be under positioned or over positioned

Similarly there should be no confused or doubtful positioning. Once a positioning has been devised, it has to be effectively communicated also in the target market.

PRODUCT LIFE CYCLE

Product life cycle displays the distinct stages in relation to the history of the product. An organization has to identify the stage in which the product or is going to be. Such an exercise helps in identifying the opportunities and problems for undertaking marketing decisions. Every product has a life cycle with distinct stages:

1) **Introduction or launch**: This stage indicates a span of slow sales, as the product is new in the market. In this stage profits are virtually non-– existent or very low.

2) **Growth:** This the stage when the product starts getting accepted in the market, sales go up, a product image is built and consequently profits go up.

3) **Maturity:** At this stage the product gets accepted by most of the targeted potential customers. Sales and profits go up till they reach a saturation point. Competition increases, market became stagnant and profits stabilize or may even decline.

4) **Decline:** In this stage, sales go down, profits go down and it is time for the organization to take hard decisions either to repackage or drop the

product. In fact, an organization should take initiate such actions at the saturation point stage itself and not wait for the declining stage.

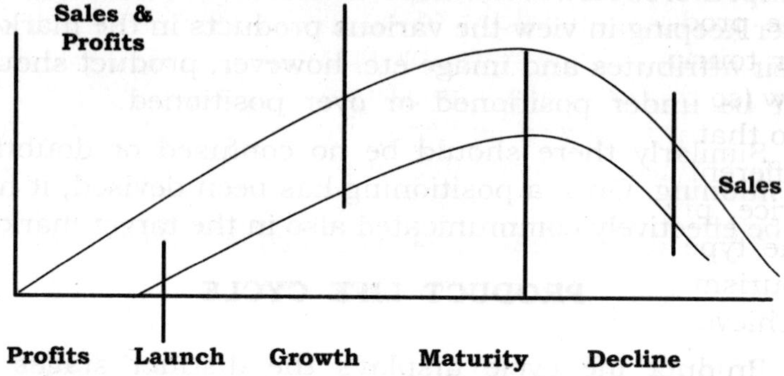

This conceptual model of product life cycle is applicable in the case of tourism products. Take for example a new hill resort. It will take certainly some time for it to become a known destination. During this period few tourists will visit it. As it becomes more known the number of visitors will increase and a stage will come when most of the tourists know about it and have paid a visit. Some among these will pay a repeat visit whereas others will look for another destination. This could be because of many reasons like after having become a popular destination it is crowded like any other mass tourist destination has lost its calm and its tranquility. However stages of life cycle vary product to product. Some may reaches at maturity stages much faster, some may take longer time

And decline fast. So a tourism marketer must observe the product life cycle so that product could be dropped or rejuvenated, alter it, improve it as new product.

Price

Price is as much a tool of marketing as promotion and plays a critical role in the marketing mix. Price conveys something to the consumer about the nature of the product or service. Pricing for tourism product should take into account the complexity created by seasonally of demand and the inherent perishability of the product. In order to be able to generate demand for tourism, price must be perceived to be neither too low (so that it denotes questionable quality) nor too high (so that it is viewed as being unaffordable. Also because different people have different perceptions about a stated price, pricing may actually become a tool in attracting the type of customer one wants to attract for a given tourism product. Pricing is ultimately only a tool to achieve overall marketing objectives.

In order to combat the twin problem of perishability of service and fluctuating demand levels tourism marketers, often resort to operations oriented pricing objectives. In such a situation essentially they vary price over time so as to ensure that demand matches available supply at any given point of time. This is done to make the most profitable use of available capacity. In addition sometimes, new entrants in the tourism market, on finding that they have slack capacities during some part of the operation cycle, may introduce special prices during the off season to maximize patronage rather than profits.

In a market characterized by tough competition, tourism organizations sometimes base their pricing decision not on their own analysis of costs and value relevant to a given pricing situation but on what competition is charging especially if they believe that price is a major determinant of consumer choice.

Owing to the highly competitive nature of the industry, discounting has become a very prevalent though controversial practice in tourism marketing. The concept of a fixed price has got limited relevance in our today's tourism marketing situation. Any discounting scheme can only succeed in pulling customers when there is some price elasticity in a given buying situation. In other words, the market is such that lower prices would attract higher number of customers and affect the quick off take of the product. The best way to hold customers is to constantly figure out how to give them more for less.

UNDERSTANDING VALUE

Value is a key concept of price, which one gets after having paid for product. The term 'value' is one that is rather loosely used. Every customer wants value in a product. Research by Zethimal found that "what constitutes value - even in a single product category- appears to be highly personal and idiosyncratic". In one of her exploratory researches, she found four broad expressions of value:

1) Value is low price,
2) Value is whatever I want in a product,
3) Value is the quality I get for the price I pay for it,
4) Value is what I get for what I give.

Value is defined on the basis of fourth category "The of all perceived benefits (gross value) minus the sum of all the perceived costs".

The greater the positive difference between perceived benefits and perceived costs, the greater the net value. If the perceived costs of using the tourism services are less than the perceived benefits its then services will possess negative net value and customer won't purchase it. When customer evaluate competing service, they are basically comparing net values. However perception are highly inaccurate, because customers may be making

These comparisons based upon very imperfect information. Further perceptions of costs and value vary widely from one customer to another and even from one situation to another.

UNDERSTANDING COSTS

As the concept of net value assessment by a customer depends upon the costs he or she may have to bear, it is important to understand the associated with a service like tourism.

There are several important costs that a potential tourist may incur in order to avail the pleasure of tourism. These may be-

1) **Monetary Cost:** which involves the actual rupee value spent on getting benefit of tourism. This is often referred to as price paid and expressed in Rupee term.

2) **Time:** Time is valuable commodity for most people, one which always has a fixed upper limit for each individual. In addition spending time for tourism involves an opportunity cost i.e. cost of the value lost had the time spent in tourism been spent in alternative gainful activities.

3) **Physical Efforts:** To a quite a lot people, physical effort entailed in getting out of their established life patterns to travel and be weary, is a substantial cost.

4) **Sensory Costs:** Travelling in addition to pleasure associated has discomforts owing to noise and pollution, unpleasant tastes, excessive climatic vagaries, uncomfortable modes of travel, in transit delays smells and sometime unappealing environment. Sometimes past experience with some of these sensory costs may actively act as an inhibitor of purchase or significantly lower the net of the package to the customer.

5) **Psychic Costs:** These are sometimes attached to the use of a service. These could be unfavorable perceptions, insecurities about certain destinations or simply a fear of taking uncertain.

Consumers, in order to determine the net value they are getting out of tourism, trade off the benefits against the costs associated with the package. The above description of costs in addition to the price undermines the fact that a reasonable price may be viewed too high if the other cost associated with a given tourism product is high and renders the "net value" and a negative gain.

Pricing theorists try to explain the concept of cost and value by saying that as all costs need to be recovered, an organization's cost of rendering of services becomes the floor below which prices can not be set as it would be non viable. Price of the product could be determined by the perceptions of the customer and competition in the market.

COST: THE INTERNAL INFLUENCE ON PRICES

Let us in this section try to understand how cost affects prices.

Gross profit for a travel agent is the difference between the prices he pays for the travel services plus his administrative costs and the price he charges the customer. The costs of a tour operator would include what he has to pay the airlines, hotels surface and local transport and other organizations providing the services that he included in the package. In addition, he has the costs of having his own organization say rants, water, and electricity and salaries of the employees and the marketing costs like advertising. These costs in accounting terminology called overhead costs as they need to be incurred even if the tour operator is not able to sell anything.

- The costs borne by tourism marketer can be understood better by classifying them into variables costs fixed costs. Variables costs are that vary directly with quantity of services produced and sold, while fixed costs do not vary with level of production is taking place or not. The total cost of a given service to any organization is a sum of fixed and variable costs attributable to that service. At the concept of break even point is simple way of understanding that how costs affect the setting up of prices. Break even point is that point in the sales of a product or service where the total revenue received from sales exactly equals the given service i.e. a situation of zero profit or loss.

Accountants also use a term contribution, which is equal to selling price minus variable costs. In case sometimes it is not possible to attract customers to cover full cost it is necessary to reduce cost of tour or tourism product which make some contribution towards on going fixed price. A good example in this tactics is provided by off-season by tourist resorts. Hill resorts during off-season offer prices that are actually below full costs, but these prices attract such people would otherwise would not have bought the service at all, at the same time make a positive contribution to the fixed costs of running these resorts during off season.

PRICES AND DEMAND

In addition to the above-mentioned concepts of costs there are two more concepts that we need to understand before getting down the exercise of price setting. These concepts are related to individual demand and elasticity of demand in relation to tourism.

1. **Individual Demand and the tourism product:** when a customer buys a tourism product, or any product, his decision partly affected by the price

of the product. Price enables customer to make a judgment about quality of the product and allows comparison with other competitor's product. In order to be able to generate demand for tourism, price must be perceived to be to be neither too low (so that it could denotes questionable quality) nor too high (so that it is viewed as being unaffordable). Pricing is actually a tool in attracting the type of customer one wants to attract for a given tourism product. You may therefore, define the kind of demand you will face by fixing up a certain level of price.

2. **Elasticity of Demand:** a change in price alone brings about a change in the level of aggregate demand is called price elasticity of demand. For example if a tour operator

Reduce the price of package tour which leads to increasing number of customer after increasing the price if customer's number falls down then it is called elasticity of demand

PRICING OBJECTIVES

Pricing is ultimately only a tool to achieve marketing objectives. Prices may be set to generate the maximum revenue or the profit to gain the largest share of a given tourism market. Once the organizations select their pricing objectives it is relatively clear to them to determine the actual figure on which they would like to sell their products.

Pricing objectives followed by tourism sector can be divided in to four categories:

REVENUE OR COST ORIENTED PRICING OBJECTIVES

The revenue oriented pricing objectives is related to make largest possible surplus, minimize costs so as to maximize returns or earn a specific target level of profits. Under this objective the tourism firm would try to follow pricing strategies that give it the maximum revenue or a certain specific return on the investment made by it. A hotel offering holiday package for example may decide to earn a 20% return on investment that it has to be made to produce those packages and thereby sets a price which would enable its return.

OPERATIONS ORIENTED PRICING OBJECTIVES

Tourism as an industry has seasonal or fluctuating demand. On the other hand tourism, because it is a service, represents a situation of perishibility of service an offer. An empty hotel room represents an unveiled services which will perish forever if it is not availed. In order to combat the twin aspects of perishbility and fluctuation of demand levels tourism marketer, often turn to operations oriented pricing objectives for hotel rooms.

DEMAND ORIENTED PRICING OBJECTIVES

This objective is depending on consumer's willingness to pay. "Demand Oriented Pricing" tries to discover through marketing research, what market is not likely to pay for the type tourism package in question. The service provider would like to charge the price, which is closest to what the market would bear. As the markets are made up of a variety of consumers, each group with a differential capacity to pay, the tourism marketer can actually use differential pricing to reach different consumer segments., specially if it is possible to create a differentiated product for each segment. Take for example Ocean liner offering cruises. All the customers are not charged the same rate, simply because all of them, apart from the basic service of the cruise, do not avail the same services. There may be deluxe and super deluxe, first class and economy class cabins, which would be accordingly priced creating differential prices for all the classes.

Differential pricing, thus, is used to enhance the total returns to the organization than what would have resulted if a simple price followed. It is also used to cope the fluctuations and seasonality of demand because, on account of perishibility, the tourism product can not be inventoried and in periods of lower demand than capacity , the available service perishes forever.

COMPETITION ORIENTED PRICING OBJECTIVES

Tourism organizations sometimes base their own pricing decisions not on their own analysis of costs and value relevant to a given pricing situation but on what competition is charging, if they believe pricing is major determinant of consumer choice. This situation is visible in airline sector, travel agency as well as the tour operators business.

In case competitions oriented pricing, generally some organizations assume the role of price leadership, where in the event of change in the cost structure for the industry, one of these organizations may raise their prices and the others follow suit. This is also referred to 'follow the leader' pricing.

PRICE SETTING RULES

The concepts of value, cost, demand and competition in the context of pricing have been discussed. Now in this section, how tourism organizations in practice make their pricing decisions, will be discussed

Markup Pricing

This the most elementary pricing method and involves adding up a standard markup to the cost of the service.

The total cost of offering the service is estimated and standard is added to this cost to arrive at the selling price. For example:

Variable cost = Rs. 3,500 per customer

Fixed cost = Rs. 50,000

Expected customers = 50

This unit costs would be given by

$$\text{Unit cost} = \frac{\text{variable cost} + \text{fixed cost}}{\text{No. of customers}}$$

$$\text{Unit cost} = \frac{3,500 + 50,000}{50} = 4,500$$

Now, assume that the tour operator wants to earn 20% markup on his sales. The prices to be charged by are given:

Markup price = unit cost

Desired return on sales

= 4,500 = Rs. 5,625/

The tour operator would charge Rs. 5,625 per person and would make a profit of Rs.1125 or 20%. The size of the markup tends to vary n the different segment of the service providers. The higher the degree of competition, the greater is the tendency to keep lower markups to attract more consumers.

Target rate of return pricing

This is another revenue overhead pricing technique, examples of which are found in the accommodation sector. The marketer tries to set a price which will yield a certain target rate of return on the investment made by the organization. The return price is determined by this formula:

$$\frac{\text{Unit cost + desired return} \times \text{invested capital}}{\text{Unit sales}} = \text{price}$$

Again in this case, marketer assuming that the customers will be willing to buy at a price that gives him a percentage of return fixes the marketer by him.

Perceived value pricing

In this market oriented technique of pricing marketer try to understand the value of his product ii the eyes of the consumers. In fact products like safari tours, adventure tours, hotels executives etc. are planned with specific consumer segment in mind, that what the consumers perceived the product and how much they can pay for the product.

Value pricing

As the competition in tourism sector companies offer value for money to the customer. They offer low prices for a reasonably good quality service.

Going rate pricing

The organization bases its prices on the basis of what the competition is charging rather than its own demand and costs. Basically it is competition oriented pricing objectives that have been discussed earlier.

Premium pricing

In this case the tourism organisation decides to sell its products above the prevailing market prices in order to have the image of high quality or to under the unique nature of its offer. A Company sets pricing according to its reputation no doubt it offers best service to the customers what they pay.

Cheap value pricing

This pricing practice is adopted to under cut the competition because of highly competitive segment of tourism market. Low or penetrative pricing is usually adopted by a new organization trying to foothold in the market or a competitor rapidly seeking his market share.

Psychological pricing

Tourism marketer sometimes applies inputs on consumer's psychology in addition to the concepts by them in their price strategy. Understanding this, tourism marketer create high quality product but often price it in a manner where high price differentiates may not be proportionate to the quality differentiate for the product offered.

Promotional pricing

Under certain circumstances tourism organizations price their product low so that they can promote demand and customers at least buy their product once may go on for repeating buying. There are some promotional pricing likes:

I. Restaurants, tour operators etc. sometimes price one of their products so that the people get exposed the product ranges attracted by the low price of the loss leader they may like to sample the other offers in the company's range of products.

II. Special event pricing: Holidays, fairs and sports events sometimes lead tourism marketer to establish special prices keeping the propensity of traveling for these activities take the advantage of these events.

III. Contract rebates whiling selling corporate packages or long term travel or tourism packages a tourism firms permits free travel on certain circuits after certain volume of business has been availed. In essence it is offering low prices for a bulk purchase to the company.

DISCOUNTING TACTICS IN TOURISM PRICING

Owing to a highly competitive nature of the tourism industry, discounting has become a very prevalent in tourism marketing. Discounting is essentially a short-term tactics that it may attract 'deal prone' consumer in a given situation. Discounts and some form of them will always prevail but constant competitive discounts would mean that overall the whole industry the whole industry is operating at lower returns. The following kinds of discounts:

I. **Discount for cash payment:** In all business transactions which operate on credit, discount is given for early settlement of in voice or different rates may be offered for cash and credit payment, the balance being the cash discount

II. **Trade discount:** These represents discounts given to people employed in the trade itself by airlines to travel agent, by hotels to airline staff, tour operators. Etc.

III. **Seasonal discount** : Perishibility of the service product is the main reason for the widespread practice of seasonal discount in the tourism sector.

IV. **Distressed stock and similar discounts:** practices such as advance and the late saver discounts are common in accommodation industry. Early bookings are beneficial to the tourism marketer as it provides them advance information about bookings. Therefore discounts are given on bookings and late saver discount is a distressed stock discount, where unsold stock needs to be cleared. This is important in tourism industry where product can not be stored.

OTHER INFUENCES ON PRICING

There are some other factors affecting the pricing decisions over which organization has little control. The important are:

I. The economic health of a given region: the economics cycles, of inflation, stagnation and depression. These are the factors which affect the demand for tourism and organization can do little about.

II. The nature of target market which is a determinant of the kind of travel product the people will buy, the prices at which they will buy, their natural propensity for travel for non business activities, the kind of holidays or destination they will choose.

III. Level of competition in the tourism market, and the substitutability of the alternative tourism package available.

Promotion

After development and bring of a product its not only make it available to target customer but also promote it among them.

In tourism, the promotion-mix are the communication efforts made by a destination or service organization to create awareness, arouse interest develop desire and persuade tourists to act and take a journey to places of attractions. All segments of the tourism industry use communication to inform and persuade customers. This communication is aimed at not only creating awareness about the product / service but also at persuading the customer to use and experience it. In other words the product/service promotion is carried through communication and certain tools are adopted for this:

- ❖ Advertising
- ❖ Direct marketing
- ❖ Sales promotion
- ❖ Public relations and publicity and
- ❖ Personal selling.

Kotler has listed certain specific tools within these categories

Advertising

Printing and Broadcast ads, packaging outer, packaging inserts, motion pictures, brochures and booklets, posters and leaflets, directories, reprints of ads, bill boards, display signs, point-of-purchase displays, audiovisual material, symbols and logos.

The objectives of communication mix or the purpose of any communication is summed in AIDA formula which is:

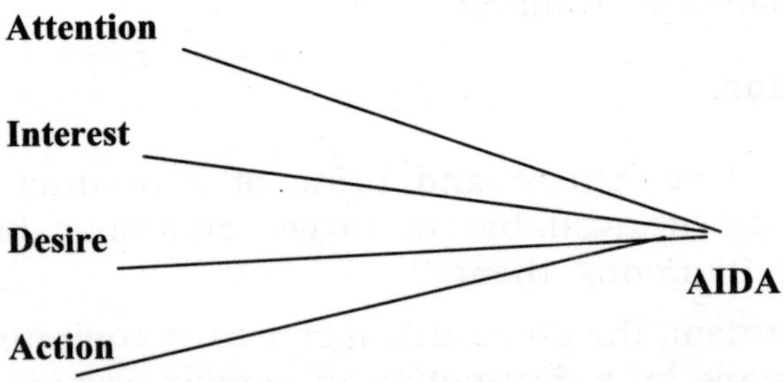

An important aspect in promotional communication is building of brand and product awareness. According to Kotler advertising is "any paid form of non personal presentation and promotion of ideas goods, or services by an identified sponsor. Advertising is done to inform or persuade the customers to try or buy a product/ service or an idea.

Public relations (PR)

Is a broader (Publicity) concept which includes publicity. Earlier marketers were using the term publicity which is now being replaced by public relations. Every organization has various internal and external groups which have an actual or potential interests in the organization. These groups are known as know publics. Public relations is important not only in obtaining editorial coverage but also in suppressing bad coverage. Personal selling is one to one / group presentation of service or product for the purpose of making sales.

There are three Cs for goods personal selling:

- ❖ Know your customer's need/desire,
- ❖ Know you company and its services and
- ❖ Know you competitors.

Sales promotion

Is short term incentive provided by any organization to customers so as to make them decide in favour of the organization. Stress given in sales promotion is for a short term and on incentives.

There are three types of sales promotion:

- ❖ Customer sales promotion (Incentives are offered to customers)
- ❖ Trade promotion (incentives are offered to middlemen)
- ❖ Sales force promotion (incentives are offered to sales people).

The broader goal of promotion is to communicate between organization and customer. Strategies used by marketer to promote product are as follows:

- ❖ **Push strategy**
- ❖ **Pull strategy**

Push strategy is whereby a supplier promotes a product to marketing intermediaries with the aim of pushing the product through the channel of distribution. For example, airlines give special incentives to travel agents for promoting their product (seats).

Pull strategy is whereby a supplier promotes a product to the ultimate customer with the aim of creating demand and thus pulling the product through the channel of distribution. For instance special discount coupons given by some hotels for promoting product. Customers are most familiar with the pull strategy.

Promotional campaign includes services or activities to achieve the desired objective. Different products and approaches to convey message to the customers. A new product may require a promotional campaign which is entirely different from an established product. The four major approaches, suggested by market experts, to develop a promotional campaign are as follows: Image Building, Product differentiation, positioning, direct response campaign.

Objective of Tourism Promotion

- To bring about the awareness among the people
- To enhance the international tourism relationship
- To earn foreign exchange and make the country economically strong
- To enhance the Regional Development
- To create the opportunity of employment

Some examples of sales promotion in travel and tourism industry are:

- Frequent Flyers Programs of Airlines.
- Incentive scheme for group travel by Airlines.
- Welcome group hotel and Indian Airlines have jointly started a scheme "We fly your spouse to you for week –end" for business executives.

- Incentive tours to Singapore/ Hongkong to travel agents and tour operators for achieving a given targeted business, etc.

FAMILARIZATION TOURS

Familiarization tours and farm trips are organized are aimed at acquainting, intimating, informing, and providing first hand experience of the products or services to the opinion makers and business providers. It is an effort by which opinion makers are to make their opinion about the merits/ demerits strength /weakness of the product and accordingly inform or influence the prospective buyers .The purpose of farm trip may vary according to:

- The aims of the organizations /destination, say the market segment an organization wants to target, and
- The stage of the product life cycle a product / destination is in . for example launch or rejuvenated stage.

Some of these purposes are:

- **Destination promotion and image building.**

Today every country /destination is making efforts to make larger share in the tourist generating market in a highly competitive market destination promotion it becomes a difficult task particularly for long haul destinations because we know services are intangibles. Therefore image building is compulsory practices in tourism industry as far as tourism product is concerned. the task of destination promotion and of image building is performed in the international markets by the national tourism organization (N.T.O.)in the domestic markets by state tourism organizations. Farm trips are regular methods applied for destination promotion and image building as the image built through the promotional effort is to be maintained, strengthened, and enhanced. For this purpose Farm trips are organized at regular intervals.

❖ **Introducing new products.**

All new tourism products howsoever attractive and strong they might be, need to be introduced / promoted at the time to the right intermediaries at the right place. for example palace on the wheels. Brochure advertisement may not yield desired result until and unless the royal grandeur is promised made to experience by the opinion makers. Try to imagine the publicity the product will get if a reputed travel magazine editor publishes a write of his /her own experience of the journey.

❖ **Damage control**

Farm trips are extremely useful for a destination / or country to deal effectively with a negative image situation. In many countries tourists arrivals suddenly drop because of crisis like health hazard, security, etc. and in such crisis the government and the industry join hands to deal with the crisis.

For example, Kargil War in India, has damage the India' s image as tourist destination for security reasons in such case opinion makers could be invited to asses the situation because India is a big country any of such crisis can not effect every part of India's security. Another example , during the 94 plague scare in India , opinion makers were invited from 30 countries to assess the situation of the country. A part from India foreign carriers like Lufthansa, Malaysian air and Air France offered free passages to India to select opinion makers so that they can give correct picture about India in their respective countries. Among the opinion makers were specialists in their respective field like 3 doctors from the world Pasteur Institute.

TRADE FAIRS AND FESTIVALS

Most of the countries are promoting special events to attract tourists organizing event oriented fem tours is a method to publicize these events. Trade Fairs are therefore means by which the practitioners of a particular sector can meet at a rallying point and watch the functioning of their peers, leaders in the sector and their competitors, regulate such a vast and definitional woolly product like tourism and encourage and develop entrepreneurial freedom.

Travel Marts is a place where the producers, sellers, and buyers (mostly intermediaries) of tourism products and services meet to face to face to transact business. It also show case the tourism product of a country or a region while also focusing on the concerns of the different sectors of the industry, like:

The issue of tariffs, clearances for investment and tax incentives, etc.

A trade fair or a travel mart is the combined effort of the seller, the buyer and the state to ensure that tourism prospers and realize the benefits that are possible.

A trade Fair or a travel mart also becomes possible when travel agents and tour operators begin to form trade and professional associations, which then can be lobby for the particular demands of the sector concerned. The major focus of the trade fair and travel mart is to give and seek information's to promote tourism both and from the region, country or a group of destinations. Thus such events attract not only the professionals but the public at large.

These events are professionally planned and organized taking into account the infrastructure, operations, and business transactions. During face to face interaction various transactions take place. For example:

- Tours are sold,
- Commissions are decided,
- Volume of business is discussed,
- Producer know the intermediaries requirements,
- Producers meet new buyer, and getting to know exercises are conducted to be followed up, etc.

Some important tourism fairs are the World Travel Market, London, the Salon Mondrai de Tourisme, Paris, The International Tourism Bourse, Berlin, Fitur, Madrid and Chicago these fairs are open to the p[professionals and the public in the main generator as well as receptor countries. India has recently started SATTE to focus on the products of South Asian region. At the 1996 Fair India, Sri Lanka and Nepal committed themselves to a joint marketing and promotion of the south Asian tourism product. They stressed the needs to foster a positive image for a region plagued by separatist and terrorist movements and talked of the needs for time to bound intra – regional movements of tourists. The buyers seller meet brought in tour operators from 40 countries to meet sellers from the region. Understanding the competitors products regarding their strength and weakness is also one of the purposes of these trade fairs.

PROMOTIONAL BUDGET

At the time of developing a workable strategy for the promotion of a product, due consideration should be given to budgeting. Whatever the amount an oragnisation can afford for promotional campaign by careful budgeting and selection of appropriate messages, media and schedule, one can effectively transmit the desired message.

The objective and task method

Under this method, the budget is based on an estimate of the amount to accomplish established objectives. Consider a promotional budget for travel agency .the task to accomplish may costs like this:

Advertising through television	Rs. 2,00,000/-
Advertisement in newspapers and magazines	Rs.1,50,000/-
Publicity	Rs. 1,00,000/-
Sales promotion	Rs.1,00,000/-
Total	Rs.5,50,000/-

Percent of sales approach

In this approach, the amount to be spent for promotion is fixed as a standard percentage of sales. Thus if a hotel desire to spend 5% of sales revenue on promotion and it expects to sell 100crore, it will allocate 5crore for promotion.

The competitive comparison method

Under this method, amount is fixed based on what competitors spend.

The fixed –sum –per –unit method

A specific amount is fixed for the promotional purpose.

These are some of the approaches to decide promotion budget. However, by having proper market information about your product and reading carefully, one can device one's own method of fixing the budget for promotion.

KEY ASPECTS OF PROMOTIONAL CAMPAIGNS

In this section, we will explain how to develop promotional campaign. Promotional campaigns include services or activities to achieve the desired objectives. Different products need different approaches to convey the messages. Because services products are intangible they need effective promotion and designing to establishing a highly competitive market or may require entirely different promotion campaign. The four major approaches to develop a promotional campaign. These are:

1) *Image building*: under this approach, emphasis is to given to communicate an image and generate customer preferences for a particular brand or company.
2) *Product differentiation*: in this approach marketer should emphasis on those aspects of the product or brand that set it apart from its competitors.
3) *Positioning*: a positioning approach promotes a brand in relation to other competitive brands in the market.
4) *Direct response campaign*: it expects a direct measurable response from the market. Personal selling activity falls in this category.

Distribution system provides the channel or means by which tourism supplier gains access to the potential customers of the product.

Victor TC Middleton has pointed out that 'The inability in travel and tourism to create physical stocks of products, adds to rather than reduces the importance of the distribution process. In marketing practice, creating and manipulating access for consumers is one of the principal ways to manager demand for highly perishable products. "Hence in relations to travel and tourism Middletown provides a definition according to which:

"A distribution channel is any organized and serviced system, created or utilized to provide convenient points of sales and /or access to consumers, away from the location of production and consumption and paid for out of marketing budget".

More than two categories of intermediaries are simultaneously used in service industry and this is particularly the case in tourism and travel industry. Following are the main function of channel members:

- ❖ Information
- ❖ Promotion
- ❖ Selling
- ❖ Financing
- ❖ Risk taking

Intermediaries increase the selling capacity of the organization by providing selling services at place, close to the customers. This also increases the geographical coverage of the market. Different intermediaries can cover various segments of the market.

DISTRIBUTION

Defination

Distribution of product or service is a mix of processes and organizations which make the product or services available to the end user. It is the flow of goods / services from the producer to consumer. Chris Cooperate listed certain aspects of tourism distribution:

- ❖ "There is no actual product which is being distributed. There are only clues given through persuasive communication about the product".
- ❖ The distribution method, "method of selling and the environment within which the purchase is made becomes part of the tourism experience."

- ❖ Travel agents dominate the distribution system by making third own decisions regarding what to display and recommend to the customers, and producers play the key role in persuasive communication as far as the distribution channels and delivery to the customers is concerned.

There are different types of distribution needs. For example in museums and monuments no prior bookings are required but queuing is used as an allocation methods for the available supply. On the other hand, in the case of trains or airlines etc., because excess demand or to ensure that one gets a seat, bookings are done in advance. The advance distribution process can be from 2 hours to 2 years or even more.

Intermediaries or middlemen commonly termed as the channel of distribution. Bucklin has defined it as "a set of institutions which performs all the activities (function) utilized to move a product a product and its title from production to consumption." over the years

The producers of services felt the need to overcome the problem of making their services available to accessible to the target to the markets. Victor TC Middleton has pointed that "inability in travel and tourism to create physical stocks of products, adds to rather than reduces the importance of distribution system. In marketing practice, creating and manipulating access for consumers is one of the principal ways to manage demand for highly perishable products." Hence, in relation to travel and tourism Middleton provides a definition according to which: "a distribution channel is any organized and serviced system , created or utilized to provide convenient points of sales and /or access to consumers, away from the location of production and consumption and paid for out of marketing budgets".

Further elaborating on this definition he stressed that:

- ❖ Channels are carefully planned and serviced by the products and not left to chance
- ❖ Each channel, once organized and serviced becomes a pipeline for the flow of sales to the target market.

We are aware that the tourism products are is rented out, consumed or experienced and there is no transfer of ownership. Intangibility, inseparability and perishiability of services make it an all together different task of designing distribution strategies for services. We will find the following differentiation between distribution of goods and that of services useful.

Goods distribution	**Services distribution**
Physical movements of goods	No physical movements of goods
Ownership is transferred to channel members	Ownership remains with suppliers of Services
Profit through resell	Commission through sales
Product manufacturing unit is	Services suppliers provide services closer also moved to market. Closer to the market.

DISTRIBUTION STRATEGY

A marketing manager has two options for distribution of the services product. Directly reaching customer and reaching customer through the middlemen. Indirect marketing would be a good strategy if the following conditions exist:

- ❖ Numbers of buyers is large,
- ❖ Frequency of purchase is high,

- Volume purchase is small,
- Market is decentralized ,
- Financial position of manufacturer is not strong,
- When manufacturer would like to share risk,
- When business is to be expanded.

The indirect marketing strategy involves use of intermediaries. They help in making the product available to consumer through the process of sharing risk and providing financial and information support. "The case for using middlemen would rest on their support efficiency in the performance of the basic marketing tasks and functions. Marketing intermediaries, trough their experiences specialization contacts and scale offer the producing organization more then it can usually achieve on its own." Direct marketing involves directly contacting the customers.

DISTRIBUTION CHANNELS

Distribution channels are different types and an organization may adopt any one type a combination of or all the types of the distribution channels. All this depends on the type of services being provided by the organization. In this section various levels of channels will be discussed:

1) *Single level channel:* Here service is directly distributed to the consumers. For examples Airlines directly booking the tickets for the customers or hotels directly books rooms for the customers.
2) *One level channel:* It implies a single where only type or category of middlemen is used. For example Airlines uses travel agents/ticketing agents for bookings for air travel. There is only one intermediary between the service supplier and the service user:

The following diagram gives the various options for using one level channel:

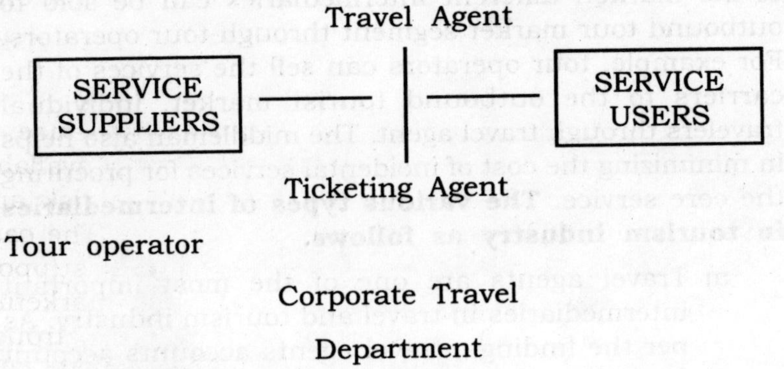

3. *Two level channel:* In this case the distribution of services is through two intermediaries. For example, in the airlines, General Sales Agent (GSA) and travel agents form two levels of distribution channel.
4. *Multi level channels:* Many time more than two categories of intermediaries are simultaneously used in service industry and this is particularly the case in tourism and travel industry. For example, the wholesale tour planner sells their services to travel agents and tour operators.

INTERMEDIARIES IN TRAVEL AND TOURISM INDUSTRY

Intermediaries basically play a very important role in travel and tourism industry. They are the resources for the organization . They provide important services in terms of financial support, information, and promotion. Information, promotion, selling, financing, and risk taking are the main functions of the intermediaries or channel members.

Intermediaries increase the selling capacity of the organization by providing selling services at places close to the customers, increases the geographical coverage of the market. different intermediaries can be sold to outbound tour market segment through tour operators. For example, tour operators can sell the services of the carriers to the outbound tourist market, individual travelers through travel agent. The middleman also helps in minimizing the cost of incidental services for procuring the core service. **The various types of intermediaries in tourism industry as follows.**

a) Travel agents are one of the most important intermediaries in travel and tourism industry. As per the findings, travel agents accounts account for 75% of domestic air travel and 90% of international air travel, 95% of international tour packages, 80% of international hotel booking and of domestic tour booking.

   These travel agents are middlemen of carriers, hoteliers, tour wholesalers etc. they get commission around 10% of service cost no charges are levied on the customers.

b) *Tour wholesaler*: tour wholesaler is the organization which plans, prepares, markets , and administers vacation and travel packages. These packages are usually a combination of the services of various suppliers like carriers, hotels guides etc.

c) Tour operator is a person or organization which operates packages prepared by tour wholesalers. Sometimes tour operators themselves provide ground services like local transport, guides' etc.

d) Corporate travel managers these are in house travel departments of large corporations. Corporate travel department provides various benefits to the organization.

- ❖ Reduces business cost,
- ❖ Enhanced services are provide,
- ❖ Increased purchasing power through bulk buying, and
- ❖ Maintains the level of quality.

e) Incentive Travel Planner often , potential travelers become confirmed ones, If they are offered some concessions. For examples in govt. or Pvt. Institutions offer leave travel commission (LTC) to make travel the employees. For these kind of traveler there are special kind of Incentive Travel Planners like I.T.D.C. in India.

f) *Consortium*: many organizations distribute their services by interacting with other orgs. consortium is the practice of offering similar service by a group of suppliers. For example the preferred Hotel World Wide is an org. with a group of more than 100 hotels. The hotels booking can be done in any of others hotel from any individuals.

g) *Franchising*: it is a hybrid form of entrepreneurship. A parent company customarily grants an individual or a company the right or privilege to do a business by using its name and by following a set of pattern of operation over a certain period of time, in a specified space.

SELECTION OF CHANNELS AND INTERMEDIARIES

Channel decision involves long term commitment and cost for the principal suppliers. In this regard the time and cost are highest as compared to any other marketing decision. Thus level of channels' selection and selection of intermediaries are a very critical to the success of an enterprise. The following factors play important role in these decisions:

- ❖ Intensity of distribution desired,
- ❖ Access to end user,
- ❖ Prevailing distribution practices,
- ❖ Revenue : Cost Analysis,
- ❖ Time horizon required for development of channel,
- ❖ Degree of control desired,
- ❖ Availability of channel participants,
- ❖ Choosing the best intermediary,
- ❖ Capability of channel participant,
- ❖ Geographical coverage desired,
- ❖ Market standing of the channel participant, and
- ❖ Financial status of the channel participant, etc.

Level of channels, selection of channel member's etc. can give results only when smooth and professional relation with intermediates are developed and maintained. There is strong interdependency between say airlines and its intermediaries like GSA ticketing agents etc.. the roles and responsibilities should be clear and specific. This Should properly spelt out in order to avoid any chances of conflict among the organization and its intermediaries. For example the percentage of commissions or royalties mode of payment, credit time etc. are decide at the initial stage it self. It is also advisable to have contracts agreements signed in this regard.

"The decision to use middle man involves the organization in a number of further decisions. The first is the problem of choosing the best middleman from the large number who are available. But might find that a desired distributor id not willing to accept the assignment. Or the distributor might handle the product only if given exclusive distribution. Or the distributor might handle the product only if it receives better financial terms than are being offered... the organization must follow this up by carefully establishing the terms and responsibilities of the distributors. This is called the trade relations mix and consists of price policies, conditions of sale, territorial rights and specific service to be perform by each party" Philip Kotler

THE FIFTH P : PEOPLE, PROCESS AND PHYSICAL EVIDENCE

INTRODUCTION

The increased attention to the application of marketing in the services sector has brought in to question what the key components or elements of a marketing mix for services, are or what they should be. If the elements chosen for a service are not comprehensive, then there could occur a gap between the market requirement and the firm's marketing offer.

This makes it appropriate to reconsider the traditional marketing mix of the 4P's in the context of marketing service. The traditional mix has been right from a mush longer list of 12 variables designed by the Harvard School of Business of time, the concept had gain acceptance and the mix adopted to capture the market.

There has always been a consistent debate on the marketing mix, and particularly in the context of services. As the 4P's model restrictive in application to the service industry, the need for including 5th P is being increasingly recognized. People, processes and physical evidence (5th P) are those elements which demand special emphasize in service marketing. This is some times considered as the separate marketing mix by it self.

OBJECTIVES

- Understand why a 5th p is necessary in tourism marketing,

- ❖ Appreciate the importance of people process and physical evidence as sub elements of the 5th P,
- ❖ Understand and appreciate the relation of this P with customer satisfaction, and
- ❖ Design strategies to make the best use of the 5P in tourism and its marketing

WHY DO WE NEED 5TH P?

In tourism marketing, the main objective is to motivate more and more people to visit different places there by enhancing the image of location/destination and also to increase the revenues. In tourism marketing, the product is intangible and it covers a vide range of facilities to the tourists.

The 4 P's are very important in tourism marketing but are not adequate. For example, there are other factors, which affect the marketing strategies like the statutory requirements to be met by the foreign nationals before entering the country, the behavioral requirements of the employees' etc. .All of which can be used effectively used in tourism marketing by effective planning all these factors need to be considered separately by paying adequate attention to each of these aspects and so can be covered under separate element of the marketing mix which may be termed as 5th P. The importance of people, process and physical evidence and their marketing implications can be studied separately under this element termed 5th P. It becomes all the important in tourism marketing to place special emphasis on it as it will help in increasing the perceived value of the product by it self. As tourism is involved in the offering of services, which lead to satisfaction of an individual need for visual delight, grandeur and exotic senses, there should be greater stress on the 5th P.

TOURISM INDUSTRY AND PEOPLE

When we talk of people here, we refer all those who are directly and indirectly employed in tourism service of the organization and who play and important role in achieving the objectives set by the firm.

People play very important role in tourism marketing. This is because customers associated people providing services as apart of the product itself. The airhostesses in Airlines and tourist guides at a historic place etc. are people who actually provide the service. They perform the following functions:

- ❖ Building and maintaining a favorable image,
- ❖ Providing solutions when problem arises,
- ❖ Providing special help in case of need, and
- ❖ Maintain harmonious relationship

PEOPLE AS AN ELEMENT OF MARKETING MIX

A few years ago, if people were spoken of as an element of marketing mix, it would have been considered blunder. But in recent times, there has been growing awareness of the role of people in achieving the marketing objectives and the importance of paying adequate attention to this aspect is being realized.

The quality of service provided can not be standardized as there is always a human element and it depends on the state of the individual at that particular moment of providing the service. This makes it difficult to control the service activities. Hence, this aspect demands serious attention to ensure a satisfied customer.

By viewing people as a separate element of marketing mix, required attention can be directed to maximize their efficiency. Steps can be taken to train people to meet the specific need of their job, motivated to have customer orientation, and reward them to make the desired contribution.

ROLES PEOPLE PLAY

The employees have to perform roles depending on the nature of job performed, their position in the organization hierarchy and the amount contacts of they have with the ultimate customers. In tourism marketing, the extent to the employees some in contact with the customers determines the amount of attention that needs to be directed to them.

People in maximum contact with tourists

They are those employees who are directly involved in tourism marketing. They include the receptionists in tourism office, tourist guides, etc. These people come in contact with a variety of potential customers who desire information and the advice on much tourism related issue. It is essential to them well versed to related destination. The package tours organized by govt. and other agencies. the probable estimates of money of money and time required for each trip, and any other information that a tourist might be interested in should be available with him.

These should well trained and motivated to serve the tourists on a day to day basis in a pleasant and responsive manner. They should be enthusiastic and friendly, with an understanding of the needs of the different people and should have the capabilities of advising them accordingly without underplaying or overplaying the importance of any particular location based on their personal bias.

People in Medium Contact with Tourists

These are people who play an important role in designing, developing, and implementing different marketing programs depending on the needs of customers.

These people have to conduct research, collect information, prepare brochures and other material for promotion and their main responsibility is to b ring the tourism marketers up to date on the latest trends.

Remember that most of the buying decision of customers are taken on basis of brochures. However, many principal suppliers are now promoting their products through video films and slides,etc.

People in Minimum Contact with Tourists

All the people who are involved in planning and development activities may not come in to contact with ultimate customers. They design attractive schemes and plan strategies for tourism- tourism development at various levels.

Coordinating the different activities of the org., internal marketing, liaison with outside agencies, etc. form the basic responsibilities at this level. Continuous feedback about the different programs and the activities is to be taken from the people who are in direct contact with the customers so as the changes desired by the public from time to time.

PROCESS IN THE TOURISM INDUSTRY

Process denotes the way in which the particular action is carried out. Tourism marketer should take care all of all the procedures, schedules, mechanisms, and routines which are practiced when the tour is on. It is at the process level that the tourists' requirements are actually met. Some of these processes are statutory in nature i.e. they required to be compiled with due to the govt. rules and regulations, while some others are practiced to facilitate easy control of the different activities. For example, Govt. may make it obligatory on the part of every tourist to furnish all full particulars of the person, nature of visit. Etc. before entering to the country.

Characteristics of processes

Any process can be analyzed in terms of its complexity and divergence. Complexity refers to the nature and sequence of the different steps of the process i.e. the variability within a process to suit the different requirements of the customers

i) **Complexity:** the wider variety of services offered by an organization the more complex it is said to be. Generally these services are provided so as to meet the needs of different segments of the customer population and aim at higher levels of penetration in a market. For example, if a tourism org, is organizing a number of package tours everyday to a different price levels to suit needs the both the economy and comfort oriented tourists, and also taking care of their accommodation and refreshment needs it is indulging in complex process.

ii) **Divergence:** divergence refers to the variability of the steps and sequences in a process. Limited divergence means the choice of a customer is restricted but it also means higher control over the quality of services provided. This may result in reduced costs, uniform service quality and improved service availability. However, as it results in highly standardized service, personal touch, which, which is desired by a number of service consumers, may be absent.

A tourist company that caters to almost any need of the customer, including helping foreign exchange transactions, flight bookings, etc. may be said to be highly divergent.

Customer Satisfaction

Processes should facilitate a service operation but at same time they should not have a negative effect on customer satisfaction. No amount of friendly approach and pleasant attitude on the part of marketing personnel will overcome continued unsatisfactory process performance. It is necessary that the processes be simplified and made customer friendly to ensure a satisfied customer.

If a service operation runs smoothly, it may not be remembered by the customer for ever, but if he/she gets dissatisfied with a process, the negative images tends to last longer. At this explains the importance that needs to be attached to the process in the tourism marketing to ensure a satisfied customer. It is difficult to have good image but easy to loose it. It is easy to earn bad image but difficult to loose it.

TOURISM INDUSTRY AND PHYSICAL EVIDENCE

Physical evidence is very much related to the product and hence is considered by many authors as a sub component of the product element and it has been argued that 'as advertising and personal selling are considered as sub elements in promotion, so as it is enough to consider physical element of product"

Tourism and physical evidence

Every customer would like to see, evaluate and compare a product physically before making a decision whether to make a purchase or not. As the services are intangible in nature, it is almost impossible to have first hand experience of the desired service before making the final purchase. How much ever a person tries to judge the quality of service by making inquiries and reading literature, a doubt still remains in mind as to them exact quality of the service to be expected.

This more true of the tourism product because a potential tourists has to estimate the amount of satisfaction he/ she derive by visiting a particular place even before deciding to go, especially, when one can choose from a number of options.

Physical evidence which can be easily associated with the by the customer. As tourism product is highly intangible, the place, the décor, the people and anything else in the tourism office may be related to the experience in store. For example, when tourists visit at Taj Mahal. They not only carry the memories of the Taj Mahal but transportation facilities, accommodation facilities available of package tour, surrounding markets and people's behavior as one whole experience. All this is a part of the conscious effort on the part of the tourist to make the intangible experience more tangible.

TYPE OF PHYSICAL EVIDENCE

Physical evidence can be divided in to two types: essential and peripheral.

a) **Essential physical evidence:** this includes al the basic requirements that are necessary to render the service. A well equipped building with all the necessary tools and information, good furniture, necessary transportation facilities to reach the area where services are provided, etc. are all essential if effective service is to be provided.

b) **Peripheral Physical Evidence:** has a little value of its own. A railway ticket has no value in itself if the traveler misses the train. This signifies that the peripheral physical evidence tries to bring an aspect of tangibility to the product but it actually represents a right to experience the service at the later point of time.

It can be understood that physical evidence tries to provide an extent of tangibility to the otherwise intangible nature of the product.

SOME C'S

Besides the Ps today certain C's have also been added in services marketing – particularly in relation to the tourism products. These are:

- *Commitment*: this means that the producer suppliers of service as well the employees must be commuted to tourism and service being provided to the tourists.
- *Cleanliness*: this is a must for destinations, hotels, airports, railways stations, and trains along with in the employees who are part of the services.
- *Communication*: this must be effective and clear with no gaps whether verbal, written or through telecommunications mode. Certain service situations require quick communication.
- *Crisis handling*: crisis in providing tourism services is not uncommon and they need careful handling.
- *Creativity*: this is the key to success in packaging or designing the tourism product.
- *Customer involvement*: a tourist not only consumes the service but also experiences it. Hence, customer involvement and participation in many tourist related services leads to enhancement of tourists enjoyment or satisfaction levels.

HISTORY OF DELHI

One of the most fascinating aspects of Delhi is the "visibility" of its historic past. Were it not for the demands of urbanization, large portions of the city could well be earmarked as archaeological parks. This is because the rulers of successive dynasties between the 13th and the 17th centuries established seven cities in different parts of Delhi. A chronological review of these cities fortunately also serves as a suitable itinerary for tourists and highlights the important monuments amongst the 1300 officially listed.

Delhi's history goes much further back in time than the 13th century. In 1955, excavations at the Purana Qila revealed that the site was inhabited 3000 years ago. Ware pottery known as Painted Gray Ware and dated to 1000 BC confirmed this as being yet another site associated with the epic Mahabharata. The excavations also cut through houses and streets of the Sultanate, Rajput, post-Gupta, Gupta, Saka-Kushan and Sunga periods, reaching down to the Mauryan era (300 BC), thus revealing almost continuous habitation. The association of Emperor Ashoka (273-36 BC) with Delhi has come to light with the discovery of a Minor Rock Edict in the locality known as Srinivaspuri.

A clearer picture of the city emerges from the end of the 10th century, when the Tomar Rajputs established themselves in the in the Aravalli hills south of Delhi. The isolated, rocky outcrop facilitated the defence of the royal resort which the Rajputs called Dhilli or Dhillika. The core of the first of the seven cities was created by Anangpal Tomar who is said to have built Lal Kot, which is the first known regular defence work in Delhi. The Chauhan Rajputs later captured Delhi from the Tomars . Prithviraj III, also known as Rai Pithora, extended Lal Kot, adding massive ramparts and gates, and made Qila Rai Pithora the first city of Delhi.

Today, only the ramparts are visible near the Qutub Minar , though the city is known to have had several Hindu and Jain temples. Prithviraj was ruling Delhi when Muhammad of Ghur invaded India, and died fighting the invader at the Second Battle of Tarain in

1192. Ghur returned, but left as his viceroy, his slave Qutbuddin Aibak.

In 1206, Qutbuddin crowned himself as the Sultan of the Slave or Mamluk dynasty, and became the first Muslim ruler of Delhi. Qutbuddin, had however, commenced his architectural career even before he chose to become the sultan. The mosque was essential to the Islamic emphasis on congregational prayer, while the burial of the dead, as opposed to cremation, introduced the tomb to India.

The earliest of these Islamic structures are to be seen in the Qutub complex and the incorporation of many Hindu elements is due to the ready availability of building material and the use of local craftsmen. Qutbuddin raised the Quwwat-ul-Islam (might of Islam) mosque, which is the earliest extant mosque in India. Within its spacious courtyard he retained the 4th century Iron Pillar, probably the standard of an ancient Vishnu temple. The pillar has puzzled scientists, as its iron has not rusted in all these centuries.

In 1199, Qutbuddin raised the Qutab Minar either as a victory tower or as a minaret to the adjacent mosque. From a base of 14.32 mtrs it tapers to 2.75 mtrs at a height of 72.5 mtrs. It is still the highest stone tower in India, one of the finest tower Islamic structures ever raised and Delhi's recognized landmark. It was completed by the Sultan's successor and son-in-low, Iltutmish. The tomb of Iltutmish, which he himself built in 1235, is nearby. Its interiors are profusely decorated with calligraphy, thought the dome has collapsed.

The Khalji rulers displaced the Slave dynasty in 1290, and when Alauddin Khali ordered renovations of the mosque in 1311, he also raised the impressive Alai Darwaza, the southern entrance to the mosque. It is the first example of a building employing wholly Islamic principles of construction, including the true arch. In

1303, Alauddin, established the second city of Delhi, called Siri, of which nothing remains but the embattlements. He also had dug a vast reservoir, Hauz Khas, to supply water to his city.

Contemporary historians describe the Delhi of that time as being the "envy of Baghdad, the rival of Cairo and the equal of Constantinople". (for the sake of convenience, tourists visiting the Qutab complex could also see the Tomb of AdhamKhan and Zafar Mahal in Mehrauli, and the Tomb of Jamai-Kamali behind the Qutb Minar. These, however, belong to a later date.) The Khalhjis were replaced by the Tughlaq dynasty in 1321. of its eleven rulers, only the first three were interested in architecture and each of them established a new city.

Tughlaqarchitecture is austere in comparison to the ornate structures raised by the Khaljis. Ghiyasuddin Tughlaq built the fortified town of Tughlaqabad, which lies 8 km east of the Qutb complex. This imposing fort is partially in ruins. It was built as a defence against the recurring invasions of the Mongols. It is still worth a visit, and the perfectly preserved tomb of Ghiyasuddin which lies to the south of the fort, is a fine example Tughlaq architecture. It once lay within a vast reservoir, was connected to the fort by a causeway and known as the Dar-ul-Aman or Abode of Peace.

Ghiyasuddin's successor, Muhammad-bin-Tughlaq built Delhi's fourth city, Jahanpanah. It largely comprised of a walled enclouser between Qila Rai Pithora and Siri. Nothing remains of it, and the Sultan is better remembered for his eccentric schemes, the most notorious of which was the transfer of the capital from Delhi to Daulatabad in the Deccan and back again to Delhi. Firoz Shah Tughlaq, a man interested in history, hunting, architecture and irrigation, created Delhi's fifth city, Firozabad. Then situated on the banks of the Yamuna, it is known as Firoz Shah Kotla. It lies of the busy Bahadur Shah Zafar Marg, Delhi's Fleet Street, and its few surviving buildings include a mosque where Timur prayed.

Of greater interest is an Ashokan Pillar. Two inscribed Ashokan pillars at Ambala and Meerut excited the curiosity of the emperor, and contemporary historians record their transportations to Delhi. One pillar was placed in Firuzabad, and it was the inscription on this one which was first deciphered by James Princep in 1837, yielding the key to the Brahmi script.

The second pillar was placed in Pir Ghaib, the emperor's hunting lodge in the Ridge. Firuz Shah extensively renovated Hauz Khas, beside which the also established a college for religious instruction and a mosque. His tomb is also there, and the village beside the impressive monuments and reservoir is now the location of boutiques and cafes. The instability which followed Firuz Shah's death was accentuated by the invasion of Timur-I-Lang (known in the west as Tamerlaine) in 1398. He plundered and laid waste the city.

Delhi's growth remained stagnant during the reign of he Sayyids and Lodis. The only interesting architectural features added by them were tomb, the best of which may be seen at the Lodi Gardens. Lady Willingdon had the area around the tomb landscaped and it remains one of Delhi's most beautiful gardens. The tomb of Muhammad Shah, the Rara Gumbad and adjoining mosque, and the tomb of Sikandar Lodi are the main monuments. A beautifully proportioned stone bridge was later built here by the Mughals.

In 1526, the last of the Lodi Sultans, Ibrahim, was defeated by Zahir-ud-din Babur, the founder of the great Mughal dynasty. The first six emperors were all extraordinary men, and their rule witnessed a powerful efflorescence of Indo-Islamic architecture and culture.

Babur chose to make Agra his capital, and it remained the Mughal capital till 1639. However, Babur's son, the emperor Humayun, built Delhi's sixth city Purana Qila, which is off Mathura Road.

The citadel was also partly raised by the Afghan Sher Shah Sur, who temporarily deposed Humayun. Sher Shah, who made a major contribution to public works, built the Qila Kunha Mosque and the Sher Mandal within the citadel in 1541. The purpose of the latter is not quite clear though it is thought that Humayun housed his library there. He fell on its steep stairs while answering the call to prayer, and died as a result three days later. Delhi's Zoological Park is adjacent to the Purana Qila.

Humayun's Tomb was raised by his widow, Haji Begum, jist 2 km south of Purana Qila. The magnificent structure in red sandstone and white marble is one of the finest examples of the garden tomb, and a precursor to the Taj Mahal. Its proportionate space, double dome and refined elegance are characteristic of Mughal architecture. Designed by a Persian architect Misak Miraza Ghiyas, it was begun in 1564 and took nine years to complete. Humayun's wives and several later Mughals are also buried within. In 1857, the last Mughal emperor, Bahadur Shah took refuge here but was captured by Lt. Hodson and exiled by the British to Rangoon. Within the spacious gardens of the tomb are a few smaller tombs and a mosque. Just across the highway from Humayun's tomb is the shrine of revered Sufi saint Hazrat Nizamuddin Auliya (d.1325). A settlement developed here during the saint's lifetime and the locality has since remained continuously inhabited. The shrine, or dargah, draws devotees from all over the Islamic world. Amir Khusrau, a poet and the saint's beloved disciple is also buried here. This locality, known as the Nizamuddin basti, is dotted with several monuments, most of which have been encroached upon. The area, however, remains a fascinating place to explore as it seems to belong altogether to another century.

In 1638, the fifth Mughal emperor, Shah Jahan decided to shift his capital to Delhi, even as he was having the Taj Mahal built in Agra. On 16th April 1639, the foundations were laid for Delhi's seventh's city on the banks of the Yamuna further north of Firoz Shah Kotla. Known as Shahjahanabad, it took nine years to complete. By 1857, this elegant capital city was all that remained of the legendary Mughal Empire. Yet, despite its periodic reversals of fortune, Shahjahanabad was never deserted. Today, it is one of the most densely populated localities in the world. Its organic growth has given it a very special character, which ahs withstood the pressures of recent times.

The capital of India has been a centre of power almost continuously since the 13th century. The huge city is divided into Old and New Delhi; the former also comprise the seventh city of the Mughals - Shajahnabad.

In 1955 excavations of the Purana Quila revealed that this area, on the banks of the Yamuna River, was inhabited more than 3000 years ago. Fine earthen pottery, known as Painted Grey Ware and dated to 1000 BC, confirmed that Delhi was associated the epic Mahabharata and Indraprastha, the capital of the Pandavas.

From the 12th to 17th centuries, the rulers of successive dynasties established seven "cities" in different parts of Delhi. The first one was with the foundation of Qutub Minar in 1199 followed by Siri in 1920; Tughlaquabad; Jahanapanah; Firuzabad, Purana Quila and Shahjahanabad.

During this period, some of the most outstanding monuments were built which stand as past glory of the

Afghan and Mughal architecture. The Qutub Minar built in 1199 rises to a height of 72.5 metres from a base of 14.32 metres; Humayun's Tomb begun in 1564 is one of the finest examples of garden Tomb, the Red Fort - an imposing citadel built in the 17th century and Jami Masjid, the largest mosque in India.

The Imperial Delhi built during the British Empire houses President's House, Parliament House, India Gate, the World War I memorial arch. Besides; Delhi offers various museums. The important ones are National Museum - the premier museum of India, National Gallery of Modern Art, Gandhi Museum Crafts Museum, Dolls Museum, Rail Museum, Temple of Bahai - a Islamic sect founded in Iran in 1836 by Bahaullah.

The streets of Old Delhi are narrow & bustling. The beauty & serenity lies inside the courts of the main buildings. Delhi has some of the finest museums in the country. Its boutiques and shopping arcades offer access to a wealth of traditional and contemporary crafts, from all over the country. New Delhi was proclaimed the capital of India by the British architect Sir Edwin Lutyens (1869-1944), & is tree-lined & spacious.

Since those early days many dynasties and rulers flourished on its regal soil. The legacy of that past survives in the many monuments left behind by the regents, each a chronicle of the glory of its time and an imprint of the character of the ruler. Today, the city is a curious blend of the modern and traditional, skyscrapers, beautiful gardens and wide tree-lined avenues perpetuate the Mughal passion of landscaping and architectural excellence. More important, however, Delhi blends within its folds the great cultural variety of India; an unceasing range of activity, a million ways of saying 'You are Welcome'.

GENERAL INFORMATION OF DELHI

Capital: New Delhi. Area: 491 sq km.

Population: 9370475.

Language: Hindi, Punjabi, Urdu, English is equally in the use.

Touring season: Oct, Nov, Feb and March. However, winter is severe and long from Nov to early March.

Climate

The summer season lasts from mid-March to the end of June, with average maximum and minimum temperatures of 36° C and 25° C. The monsoon season, following the hot summer, continues until the end of September, with an average rainfall of about 26 inches. The winter season extends from late November to mid-February. The coldest month is January, when both the mean maximum temperature and the mean minimum temperature are at their lowest—21° C and 7° C, respectively.

TRANSPORTATION

Air

Delhi is the main gateway city for northern India with a modern airport. All major international air carriers operate direct services to Delhi from various centres in the world.

Delhi is the base for Indian Airlines operations in North India and the airline connects the city with all major centers of tourist and business interest in the country.

Indira Gandhi international Airport is divided into two wings, International Terminal (20 km from downtown Connaught Place) and Domestic Terminal

(15 km from City Centre).

Taxi and coach transfer is available from both International and Domestic Arrivals. Pre-paid Taxi (a service with journey fare paid at the booking counter), air-conditioned and non- air-conditioned coach counters are located immediately outside the customs Hall in International Terminal and outside Baggage Claim area in Domestic Arrivals.

Airport Coach (non-air-conditioned) is operated by Delhi Transport Corporation (via Connaught Place and Railway Stations) to Inter State Bus Terminus (ISBT), Kashmiri Gate and by Ex- Servicemen's Air link

Transport Service to Connaught Place. The coach covers all major hotels enroute

Rail

Delhi is the hub of the Indian Railways network with Express trains to all parts of the country. Shatabdi Express air-conditioned fast tourist train operates to Bhopal (via Agra, Gwalior, Jhansi), Luckhnow (via Kanpur) and Chandigarh, and provides access to some of the neighboring tourist centres.

Delhi is serviced by two lines, broad and meter gauge and has three major railway stations, Delhi Main (receives both broad and meter gauge trains), New Delhi and Hazrat Nizamuddin. Delhi Main Railways Station is 6 km from Downtown, New Delhi is about 1 km and Nizamuddin 5 km.

Taxis, auto rickshaws, cycle rickshaws and city Bus Service are available at the railway stations for transfer. Delhi Transport Corporation (DTC) operates special services from railway stations to different parts of the city.

Computerized Railway Reservation Offices:

- IRCA Building, Chelmsford Road, Pahar Ganj, New Delhi. (0745-2100 hrs; Sunday 0745-1400 hrs)
- Delhi Main Railway Station. (0745-2100 hrs; Sunday 0745-1400 hrs)
- Delhi Shahdara Railway Station. (0745-2100 hrs; Sunday 0745-1400 hrs)
- Sarojini Nagar Railway Station. (0745-2100 hrs; Sunday 0745-1400 hrs)
- Near Hazrat Nizamuddin Railway Station. (0745-1300 hrs and 1400-2000 hrs; Sunday 0745-1400 hrs)
- Kirti Nagar Railway Station. (0745-1300 hrs and 1400-2000 hrs; Sunday 0745-1400 hrs)
- Karkardooma, Har Govind Enclave, Vikas Marg. (0745-1300 hrs and 1400-2000 hrs; Sunday 0745-1400 hrs)
- International Tourist Bureau, 1st Floor New Delhi Rly. Station, Tel.: 3734164; 0730-1700 hrs. Closed on Sunday. (0745-1300 hrs and 1400-2000 hrs)

Bus

Delhi is linked by bus services, air-conditioned, deluxe and ordinary, to all major destinations in north India. Delhi Transport Corporation and Road Transport Corporations of neighboring States provide frequent bus services.

Inter State Bus Terminus, the focus of all inter-city bus services, is located at Kashmiri Gate, 7 km from Downtown. Taxis, auto and cycle rickshaws, City Bus Service and Night Bus Services are available at the ISBT for transfers.

ISBT General Enquiry, Tel.: 2519083

Delhi Transport Corporation (DTC), Tel.: 2518836

Haryana Roadways, Tel.: 2521262

Punjab Roadways, Tel.: 2517842

Himachal Road Transport Corporation, 1 Rajpur Road, Tel.: 2516725

Rajasthan Roadways, Bikaner House, Pandara Road, Tel.: 3383469

U.P. Roadways, Ajmeri Gate, Tel.: 3315367, 2518709.

Road

Road distances from Delhi to some important tourist centres in the region:

Agra 200 km ; Ajmer 389 km; Amritsar 446 km; Bharatpur 190 km; Bhopal 741 km; Chandigarh 249 km; Corbett National Park 270 km; Gwalior 319 km; Jaipur 261 km; Jammu 586 km; Jodhpur 104 km; Kota 505 km; Lucknow 509 km; Pathankot 478 km; Shimla 343 km; Srinagar 876 km; Udaipur 663 km; and Varanasi 797 km.

LOCAL TRANSPORT

Delhi offers a variety of public transport. Yellow-top taxis and auto-rickshaws (seats three) are available everywhere. Cycle-rickshaws, mostly used in Old Delhi areas, rates negotiable.

DTC operates an extensive network of city bus service covering all areas of the city and suburbs, The city also operates pollution-free battery operated buses between Connaught Place and Chandni Chowk and along Chandni Chowk. In case of complaints against taxi or auto-rickshaw for overcharging or cheating, note down the number of the vehicle and lodge a report with Deputy Commissioner of Police (Traffic), M.S.O. Building, Indraprastha Estate, Tel.: 331 8840, or the nearest traffic policeman.

ACCOMMODATION

- Ashok, 50-B, Chanakyapuri.
- The Surya, Friends Colony. Tel.: 6835070, Fax: 6837758. 236 rooms.
- Centaur, Indira Gandhi International Airport.
- Claridges, 12 Aurangzeb Road.
- Hotel Inter-Continental New Delhi, Barakhamba Avenue, Connaught Place,
- Tel.: 3320101, Fax: 3325335. 444 rooms.
- Hyatt Regency, Bhikaji Cama Place, Ring Road.
- Imperial, Janpath.
- Le Meridien, Windsor Place, Janpath, Toll Free No. 1600131415
- Fax: 91-11-371 4545. 355 rooms.
- The Park, 15 Parliament Street, New Delhi - 110 001 Tel.: 3733737 Fax: 3732025, Telex: 031 65231.
- Qutab, Sri Aurobindo Marg.
- Hotel Samrat, Chanakyapuri, Tel.: 6110606, Cable: HOTEL SAMRAT, Fax: 6887047, 4679056. 247 rooms.
- Siddharth, 3 Rajendra Place.
- Taj Mahal, 1 Mansingh Road.
- Taj Palace, 2 Sardar Patel Marg, Diplomatic Enclave.
- The Oberoi, Dr. Zakir Hussain Marg, Tel: 4363030, Fax : 4360484. 287 rooms.
- Vasant Continental, Vasant Vihar.
- Welcomgroup Maurya Sheraton Hotel & Towers, Diplomatic Enclave, Tel.: 6112233, Fax: 6113333.

- ❖ Ambassador, Sujan Singh Park, Tel.: 4632600, Cable: HOTEL AMBASSADOR, Telex: 031-74045, Fax: 4632252. 88 rooms.
- ❖ Connaught Palace, 37 Shaheed Bhagat Singh Marg.
- ❖ Hotel Diplomat, 9 Sardar Patel Marg, Tel.: 3010204, Cable: DIPLOMATIC, Fax: 3018605, 25 rooms.
- ❖ The Hans Plaza, 15 Barakhamba Road, Tel.: 3316861 to 3316868, Fax:3314830.
- ❖ Hotel Janpath, Janpath, Tel.: 3340070, Cable: RESTWELL, Fax: 3347083, 3368618. 213 rooms.
- ❖ Marina; G-59 Connaught Circus.
- ❖ Nirula's, L-Block Connaught Circus.
- ❖ Oberoi Maidens, 7 Sham Nath Marg.
- ❖ Rajdoot, Mathura Road.

OTHER HOTELS

- ❖ Nest, Corner House, 11 Qutab Road, Ram Nagar.
- ❖ Rail Yetri Niwas, Gate No. 2 New Delhi Railway Station.
- ❖ Railway Retiring Rooms: Available at both New Delhi 8 Old Delhi Railway Station They are allotted to Railway passengers in 1st come 1st serve basis. Tourist Camping, Park, J.N. Marg.
- ❖ Vishwa Yuvak Kendra, Circular Road, Chanakyapuri.
- ❖ Y.M.C. A Tourist Hostel, Jai Singh Road.
- ❖ Youth Hostel, 5 Nyaya Marg, Chanakyapuri.
- ❖ Y.W.C.A., Blue Triangle, Ashok Road.
- ❖ Y.W.C.A. lntenational Guest House, 10 Sansad Marg.

- Airport Retiring Room: Term-l.
- Reservation Authority, Airport Manager Delhi Airport 1st come 1st serve basis with confirmed tickets only if flying out of the country within 24 hrs., Tel.: 5652021, 5662011.
- Alka, 16/90 P Block, Connaught Circus. Tel.: 3344328, Cable: HOTELALKA, Fax: 351796. 23 rooms.
- Ashok Yatri Niwas, 19 Ashok Road.
- Bhagirath Palace, Chandni Chowk.
- Broadway, 415A, Asaf Ali Road.
- Fifty Five, H-55 Connaught Circus.
- Flora, Dayanand Road, Darya Ganj.
- Lodhi, Lala Lajpat Rai Marg.
- Manor, 77 Friends Colony.
- Ranjit, Maharaja Ranjit Singh Road.
- Regal, 4815 Shyama Prasad Mukherjee Marg.
- Sartaj, A-3 Green Park.
- Shiela, Pawha House, Qutab Road, Ram Nagar.
- Sobti, 2397 Hardhian Singh Road, Karol Bagh.
- Tera, 2802 Bara Bazar, Kashmiri Gate.
- Vikram, Mahatma Gandhi Marg, Lajpat Nagar.
- York, K-Block Connaught Circus.

PLACES OF INTEREST

Delhi- the commercial hub has many tourist attractions to offer. Visit vibrant shopping complex of Connaught Place, Delhi Haat for handicraft goods and delicious food bonanza. Pay a visit to Red Fort and Qutub Minar to view the excellence of Mughal architecture.

Or just drop in at Janpath- for buying a variety of cheap and best items. If you are looking for spiritual peace, visit Lotus temple, which is also famous for its marvelous architecture and heavenly beauty. Take a stroll at Rajpath. Or pay a visit to India Gate and Rashtrapati Bhawan for viewing monuments made during British era.

Remnants of the glorious past survive cheek - by - jowl with soaring skyscrapers, posh residential colonies and bustling commercial complexes. Delhi has some of the finest museums in the country. Its boutiques and shopping arcades offer access to a wealth of traditional and contemporary crafts, from all over the country.

Delhi has specialty restaurants to please the gourmet, sprawling parks and gardens ablaze with flowers, and in the winter months, a variety of cultural events. The myriad faces of the city are simply tantalizing, and entice the curious traveller into a fascinating journey of discovery.

Chandni Chowk - One of the main markets of Delhi, Chandni Chowk was once lined with beautiful fountains.

But today the place is very crowded and congested. Chandni Chowk is located opposite the Red Fort. The Area has got the Digamber Jain Temple which houses the Birds hospital. On one end of Chandni Chowk is the Fatehpuri Mosque which was erected by the wives of Shah Jahan. Opposite the old police station or the Kotwali is the Sunheri Masjid from where Nadir Shah ordered his troops to plunder and massacre Delhi.

Dilli Haat

An exclusive upgradation of the traditional 'haat'. Dilli Haat is the first ever permanent fair for crafts, food and cultural activities in India. The craftsmen from all over the country and the cultural happenings provide a panoramic view of the richness and diversity of Indian handicrafts and artefacts. Dilli Haat also houses food stalls serving a variety of traditional food from different parts of India.

Connaught Place (Rajiv Gandhi Chowk)

Built by the British, Connaught Place is quite close to the New Delhi railway station and a unique shopping spot. Palika Bazaar another famous underground shopping centre is located here.

Humayun's Tomb

Built for his wife of Humayun, Haji Begum in the mid 16th century, and this red sand stone structure is considered to be the predecessor of Taj Mahal. The structure is one of the best example of Mughal Architecture. Humayun's wife is also buried in the red and white sandstone, black and yellow marble tomb. The entry in the complex is free on Fridays otherwise a nominal fees of .50 ps is charged

Jantar Mantar

Few minutes walk from Connaught Place is is a strange collection of solomon coloured structures. These were built by Maharaja Jai Singh and is actually an observatory. Though not as large as its compatriot in Jaipur Jantar Mantar at Delhi also an attraction for the tourists. The astonishing part of these observatories is that they can calculate many astronomical movements very accurately.

Red Fort

Built in Red Sand stone this imposing fort is 3 kms in perimeter with the height of the wall varying from 18 to 30 meters at places. When the Red fort was being built Yamuna used to flow on its one sides and there were deep moats on the other. Today Yamuna flows almost a kilometer away from the fort and the moats have dried up. In the evening the Delhi Tourism organizes a light and sound show which narrates the history of Delhi

Qutab Minar

In 1199, Qutbuddin raised the Qutab Minar either as a victory tower or as a minaret to the adjacent mosque. From a base of 14.32 mtrs. it tapers to 2.75 mtrs. at a height of 72.5 mtrs. It is still the highest stone tower in India, one of the finest stone tower in India, one of the finest Islamic structures ever raised and Delhi's recognised landmark. It was completed by the Sultan's successor and son-in-law, Iltutmish. The tomb of Iltutmish, which he himself built in 1235, is nearby, Its interiors are profusely decorated with calligraphy, though the dome has collapsed.

India Gate

A majestic arch, 42 metre high, is a war memorial in honour of the Indian soldiers who died during the First World War. The eternal flame (Amar Jawan Jyoti) burns beneath the arch to honour the memory of the unknown soldiers.

Lakshminarayan Temple

A modern Hindu Temple built in 1938, is dedicated to Lord Vishnu and his consort Laxmi

President's House

This palace like building was build by the British with a blend of Mughal and Western culture. It is now the official residence of the President of India.

Parliament House

This impressive collonaded building houses the two houses of Parliament

National Museum

It houses an excellent collection of bronzes, terracotta sculptures, paintings and costumes.

Jantar Mantar

This Unique observatory was built by the Rajput King Sawai Jai Singh II in 1724. It was believed to have been built with machinery instruments for observing the movement of stars and planet.

Raj Ghat

The serene memorial of Mahatma Gandhi on the banks of Yamuna

Shanti Vana

The cremation site of Jawaharlal Nehru.

Jama Masjid

It was built as the mosque of Shahjahan's capital city in 1658 and is the biggest in India

Old Fort

This fort was built by Sher Shah in the 16th Century

Bahai Temple

Situated atop the Kalka hill, this distinctive lotus shaped marvel in marble is surrounded by a landscaped garden

Teen Murti House

The erswhile residence of Jawaharlal Nehru, India's first, Prime Minister, is now a museum. A son et lumiere is held here

Tughlaqabad Fort

Its massive ramparts can be seen from a distance. Built in the early 14th century, this stark and powerful fortress palace was built by the first Tuglaq King and has 13 gates. Also nearby is Suraj Kund, famous for its hot-water well

GARDENS IN DELHI

Moghul Gardens - The Mughal Garden

Is located in the premises of the President house. This garden is not opened to public viewing. During the spring seasons of February and March, when the garden is in full bloom people are allowed inside. This garden have some exotic and rare flower plants. The dwarf orange trees and numerous Rose plants are special attraction in the garden. The fountains add to the beauty of the place.

Rose Garden - National Rose Garden is situated in the Chanakya Puri area of the capital. This garden has some of the rare and imported rose variety. The best season to visit this garden is during December / January when the flowers are in full bloom.

MUSEUMS IN DELHI

National Rail Museum - National Rail Museum is located In Chanakya Puri. It is unique in its collection of rail engines and locomotives. India was among the countries which had railway lines since 19th century.

The locomotives in the museums are displayed in open. But they also have a small in house museum which gives the details of the progress and development in the history of railway in India.

National Museum - Located on Janpath, National museum is one of the treasure houses of the our glorious past. The museum has a large collection of excavated items many of which date back to 2nd and 3rd century B.C. The museum has separate section for the Harrapa (Indus valley civilisation) collection.

Nehru Museum & Planetorium - The Teen Murti house was the residence of India's first Prime minister Pt. Jawaharlal Nehru. After his death the house was converted into a memorial. The Nehru memorial has a collection of gifts and many other items which he possessed. Nehru Planetorium is within the compound of Teen Murti. This planetorium gives a overview of the Indian Space program. There are daily film shows which are screened in a specially designed auditorium. These films are meant to give information about the Universe or any other topic related to that. The Capsule in which Rakesh Sharma went into space is also kept here.

Dolls Museum - A unique museum of Dolls is located near the ITO crossing on the Bahadur Shah Jafar Marg. These dolls are collected from different parts of India as well as from other countries of the world. These dolls reflect the tradition and culture of the region from where they come.

Food

From age - old eateries in the by lanes of the Walled City to glitzy, specialty restaurants in five - star hotels, Delhi is a moveable feast. It offers a choice of Indian and international cuisines in different ambiences to suit varied budgets.

For gourmets, Delhi is synonymous with Mughlai and Frontier cuisines. The best of Mughlai cuisine can be enjoyed at Karim, (both in Jama Masjid and Nizamuddin) where recipes, dating from the times of the Mughals have been the closely - guarded secret of generation of chefs.

Delhi Ka Aangan (Hyatt Regency), Darbar (Ashoka Hotel) and Corbetts (Claridges) are among the many options available in the expensive range, while Gulati Restaurant (Pandara Market), Angeethi (Asiad Village) and Degchi (Regal Building) are among those catering to more modest budgets. The finest Frontier cuisine is available at the Bukhara (Maurya Sheraton), Frontier (Ashoka Hotel) and Baluchi (The Hilton).

At the other end of the scale are many popular road side eateries around Jama Masjid and Nzamuddin where kababs, rotis and biryani are order of the day. Every five - star hotel in the city has a Chinese restaurant, while most markets in South Delhi have a medium - budget Chinese restaurants. The popularity of this cuisine can be gauged by the immumerable Chinese food outlets of the "meals- on - wheels" and kiosk variety.

The growing sophistication Delhite's palate is discernable in the increasing number of speaciality restaurants- EI Arab (Regal Building), Dum Pukht or the process of slow cooking developed in Awadh (Maurya Sheraton), Kashmiri food at Chor Bizarre (Hotel Broadway), Thai food at Baan Thai (The Oberoi) and Sukothai (Hauz Khas Village), Japenese food at Tokyo (Ashoka Hotel) and Osaka (Hauz Khas Village), Tibetan food at eateries near Chanakya Theatre, and Mexican food at Rodeo (Connaught Place).

Another indication is the frequency and popularity of food festivals organised by Hotels. South Indians food is another favorite, the vegetarian variety of which is best in enjoyed at Sagar (Defence Colony), Sagar Ratna

(Lodhi Hotel) and Dasaprakash (Hotel Ambassador). Coconut Grove (Ashok Yatri Niwas) offers excellent non-vegetarian cuisine from South India.

The best of continental cuisine can be eaten at five - star hotels, for instance La Rochelle (The Oberoi), The Orient Express (Taj Palace) and Captains Cabin (Taj Man Singh), though numerous multi - cuisine restaurants also offers continental food. Keeping pace with the changing face of the city are the growing number of fast food outlets which serve all manner of cuisines.

A delightful outlet offering a range of Indian cuisines are the food stalls ar Dilli Haat, here, the cuisine of different states is made available at very moderate rates. Set in the mindset of a spacious crafts bazaar these cafes are a very pleasant place to enjoy food.

For the more intrepid, eateries such as those at Paranthe wali gali, or chaat at Bengali Market and Sunder Nagar, bhelpuri at Greater Kailash and sweetmeats from Annapoorna and Ghantewala can be part of the gastronomical tour of Delhi.

Delhi is also synonymous with the omnipresent tandoori chicken and tandoori roti, which, when freshly had from the tandoor, makes a delicious meal. This is often available at roadside dhabas at a moderate cost.

SHOPPING

Delhi is a veritable paradise for shoppers, who can buy objects ranging from the simplest of Indian handicrafts to international designer labels, and often within the same shopping area.

Delhi is unique in that it has representative outlets for the handicrafts of each Indian state. This in it self presents a staggering array of goods, and at very affordable prices. In the last decade there has been a dramatic change in Delhi's markets. Upwardly mobile lifestyle has led to greater sophistication in display and upgrading of various markets in terms of availability of items.

Delhi has long been the most important trading centre in Northern India. Many of its localities, like Sheikh Sarai and Yusuf Sarai, derive their names from medieval market towns which serviced the bygone, shifted capital cities of Delhi. Today, all of these have become a part of the rapidly expanding metropolis. Instead of market towns, there are specific whole sale markets or"mandi's" scattered throughout the vast city.

For visitors to Delhi, shopping is high on the list of "things to do". Tourists find a wide choice of items-such as carpets, silks, jewellery, leather and silver ware, handicrafts and hand printed cotton - that are synonymous with India. Each item is available in a range of prices, depending on the quality and the outlet.

Another interesting is that each market has its own, distinctive ambience and adds its own flavour to the experience of shopping. Haus ·Khas Village, Connaught Place and Chandni Chowk are worlds apart from one another, yet each of them reflects an aspect of this many - faceted city. In fact one of the fascinating ways of understanding a city is by wandering through its market places for it is here that contemporary culture is most visible to the outsider.

The exploration of Delhi's markets could be beginning at Chandni Chowk. Despite the pressures of traffic and population, its historic land marks service to tell the story of the last three centuries. Many of the shops here are more than 100 years, old and the mesh of lanes and by lanes is full of supervises. Leading off Chandni Chowk are Dariba, the silver market, Khari Baoli, the spice market and Kinari Bazar for trimmings and tinsel. In some of these bazaars the item for sale are manufactured at site, which lands a special charm to the shopping experience well integrated into the culture of the old city, these bazaars offer the visitor a glimpse of life in Old Delhi.

There are some antique stores behind Jama Masjid, and more lining the entrance to the Red Fort, where the Meena Bazar once was. These offer items arranging from jewellery to painting and furniture, and cater almost entirely to tourists. Connaught Place, New Delhi's original shopping arcade was planned as part of the Imperial capital in 1911. On Baba Kharak Singh Marg, are the numerous government State Emporia. Which afford a glimpse of the handicrafts of each state. So does the recently- inaugurated new Central Cottage Industries Emporium on Janpath. Across the road from "Cottage" as it is popularly known, are the inviting stalls along Janpath.

The Tibetans sell jewellery and ritual objects, while closer to Connaught Place are available embroideries from Gujarat and Rajasthan, readymade garments and bric- a - brac. When the weather is good it is pleasant to amble down Janpath, where bargaining is the order of the day. Sundernagar Market is a fine place to shop for antiques and silver jewellery. The well - appointed stores keep a choice selection, especially of silver jewellery from Ladakh, semi- precious stones, some textiles and brass, copper and silver object d'art.

Not far from Sundernagar is the Crafts Museum Shop, attached to the museum in Pragati Maidan. Moving further south are the up market shopping centers of South Delhi- South Extension, Greater Kailash I and II, Green Park and Hauz Khas Village.

The haunt of the nouveau riche, these markets offer a combination of ethnic chic and designer lebels, Indian and international. Hauz Khas Village has set a very interesting trend as market. Over the countries, a village had developed around the medieval college and the tomb of Firoz Shah Tughlaq. A few years ago, an association called Dastakar - set up a showroom in the village. Now the village has a plethora of boutiques, galleries and restaurants which coexist with the buffalos, cow pats and men smoking hookahs on charpoys. Far from being a deterrent, the "rural" ambience is a positive attraction.

Other villages like Mehtauli, Khirkee and Lado Serai are fast following suit. Seeing the popularity of crafts bazaars held periodically in the capital, Delhi Tourism has set up a permanent outlet for craftsperson's at Dilli Haat, where space and the availability of Indian cuisines make the visit a very pleasant experience. A more up market outlet for Indian handicrafts and antiques is the bazaar near the Qutab Minar.

The Santushi Shopping Arcade opposite the Ashoka Hotel has become another popular up market haunt. Developed by the Air Force Wives Association, it has a select number of boutiques where apparel, furnishings and accessories are available. A restaurant and patisserie add to the quiet charm of the place.

FESTIVALS IN DELHI

Delhi's festival calendar begins with the Republic Day parade on 26th January. It is the most colorful of the city's festivals events and also the biggest crowd-puller. Hundreds of thousands people line the route from Rajpath to the Red Fort to watch the pageant of solders, camel crops, armored regiments, brass bands, folk dancers, school children, war veterans and elaborate floats representing the cultural diversity of India. The two hour long parade is usually rounded off with a much-awaited spectacular fly - passed presented by Air Force squadrons. A special display of folk dances also takes place at the Talkatora Stadium. Three days later the Beating of the Retreat takes place at Vijay Chowk. Various bands of the armed forces set the pace for marching troops against the grand backdrop of Rashtrapati Bhawan.

In a much lighter vein, winter also witnesses the Vintage Car Rally when the 'grand old ladies', spruced up for the occasion, make the long haul from Delhi to Sohna. Winter is also the time for the popular Balloon Mela, the Surajkund Crafts Mela on the outskirts of Delhi, and Delhi Tourism's Gardens Festivals. The latter is a visual feast, for Delhi a blaze with flowers in the month of February Delhi Tourism also organizes cultural performances during the Garden Festivals.

Holi, the festivals of colors, marks the onset of spring. In August, the festival Janamashtami, celebrates the birth of Lord Krishna. Ballets in the Kathak dance style depict the life of Lord Krishna.

In early October, a festival specific to Mehrauli, in Delhi, takes place. This the Phulwalon - Ki - Sair or the Flower sellers Procession, which originated in the 16th century. The highlight is a prossional of people carrying decorated floral fans, which are blessed at the shrine of the 13th -century Sufi saint, Khwaja Qutbuddin Bakhtyar Kaki and at the hindu temple of Jogmaya, both in Mehrauli. The procession ends with a formal ceremony at the Jahaz Mahal, a 16th - century pleasure resort by the side of a lake.

Also in October is Dussehra, commemorating the victory of Lord Rama over the demon king, Ravana. A month - long Ram Lila dance festival is organized by the Bhartiya Kala Kendra, depicting seems from the epic Ramayana, while on Dussehara evening itself, gigantic effigies of Ravana are set a fire. The biggest venue for this event is the Ram Lila ground, of Asaf Ali Road. Delhi Tourism organizes the popular Qutab Festival in October. Musicians and dancers performs at night by the city's 12th -century land mark, the Qutab Minar.

Diwali, the festivals of lights is preceded by several Diwali Melas, where food, handicrafts and a variety of earthern lamps and candles are sold. Large communities of Indians from different states reside in Delhi. As a result, regional festivals are also celebrated in the capital.

Arts & crafts

As the seat of empires for centuries, and with royalty as patrons, Delhi has long been a cultural center, attracting the best of painters, musicians and dancers. Though today's patrons have changed, Delhi is more than ever the cultural capital of the country, and is also visited by foreign dancers, musicians and theatre groups en route to the Far East.

October to March is the "cultural season" of Delhi, during which time a plethora of events take place in the fields of the visual and performing arts. The best of the performing arts representing the range of classical dance forms and schools of music from all over India can be viewed at Kamani Auditorium, the Chamber Theatre at Triveni Kala Sagam, FICCI Auditorium, the India International Center, Siri Fort, LTG Auditorium, Pragati Maidan and Sri Ram Centre, where Delhites can enjoy the privilege of seeing, and listening to, the legendary gurus as well as their disciples.

Music lovers look forward to the Shankarlal, Dhrupad and Tansen Festivals in February and March and the Vishnu Digamber Festival in August, at which India's greatest musicians perform Roshanara Festivals of music and dance organized by Delhi Tourism.

October witnesses the popular Qutub Festivals where reputed musicians and dancers offer captivating renditions with the Qutub Minar as the backdrop. Film buffs eagerly await the National Film Festivals and the bi-annual International Film Festival, held in January. Apart from commercial cinema houses, films are periodically screened at the Max Mueller Bhawan, the Alliance Francaise, the Japan Cultural Centre, the

British Council Division, the Russian Centre for Science and Cultural and the Hungarian Information Centre,

Theatre in Delhi receives a constant impetus from the presence of the National School of Drama. The variety offered ranges from Hindi translations of European plays, to regional theatre, as well as folk forms. Delhi's numerous art galleries reflect the country's burgeoning art scene. Well-known and new artists from all over the country display their works in these galleries. Notices of exhibitions are given in daily newspapers and specific city magazines.

Among the active galleries are Art Heritage, Triveni Art Gallery, Sridharani Gallery, Art Today, Vadehra Art Gallery, Eicher Gallery, Gallery 42, Dhoomi Mal Art Centre, Gallery Escape, Lalit Kala Akademi, LGT Gallery, Gallery Ganesha, Gallery steps, AIFACS, Max Mueller Photo Gallery, British Council Divisio Gallery, Gallery Romain Rolland, Khirkee Gallery, the Village Gallery and at times the American Centre.

Traditional crafts, too have long been practiced in Delhi. The city was particularly well known for its silver and gold enameling, and zari or embroidery in gold thread. Master-crafters men in both crafts still live in the Walled City where there are also miniature painters.

Delhi also has fine potters, wooden toy makes, kite makers and lacquer craftsmen. In Old Delhi it is not unusual to come upon a traditional workshop.

The wealth of Indian handicrafts can be enjoyed at the Crafts Museum at Pragati Maidan, at the State Emporia on Baba Kharak singh Marg, and at Dilli Haat, which is Delhi Tourism's popular venue for crafts bazaars throughout the year.

DELHI A TOURIST DESTINATION

The city has exploded in all directions beyond the confines of Lutyens's wide, tree-lined avenues, with an exuberance that is characteristically Indian. Several factors have contributed to this breathless pace of growth. For North India, especially, Independence also meant Partition.

In 1947, many Muslims Families of Delhi migrated to Pakistan while many Hindus and Sikhs from west Punjab sought refuge in the city. They were given land west of the Ridge and south of New Delhi. Many of these refugees also their houses across the Yamuna and north of Shahjahanabad. Since, then, the influx into the city hasn't ceased. The manpower required by the government in the capital is itself staggering.

Industrialists, entrepreneurs and migrant labor from all over India have turned to Delhi in search of livelihood and success, and made it a commercial capital as well. The cultivated fields which till recently could be seen on the outskirts of the city, have been developed into residential colonies and commercial complexes. High-rise buildings now stand cheek - by - jowl with Delhi's 1300 monuments. Villagers such as Khirkee, Begumpur, Hauz khas, Sheikh Sarai and Nizamuddin which grow around medieval Delhi's shifting capital 'cities', have now been engulfed by the urban sprawl. Many of them, however, retain their old-world characteristics.

The line of distinction between Old and New Delhi had begun to blur- north; south, east and west Delhi are more prevalent terms of demarcation. The facilities and opportunities available in Delhi have attracted Indians from far- flung corners of the country, making it a melting pot of sorts. On the other hand, the presence of diplomatic and trade missions, the growing number of multi-national companies and foreign investors, and the influx of tourists and visiting professionals have given the city, especially its southern and central parts, a cosmopolitan air. The coexistence of the past and the present at many levels characterizes Delhi, as it does India.

The assimilation of a specific cultural influence is expressed differently by people living in different parts of the city, a fact that offers insights into the social strata. South Delhi is undoubtedly the trend - setter, and the fashions and lifestyles introduced here become the aspiration of many.

There are however, dramatic differences in localities, standards of living and adherence to traditions. Delhi is one of the most historic capitals in the world and two of its monuments- the Qutab Minar and Humayun's Tomb- have been declared World Heritage Sites. It is also one of the greenest capitals for the visitor, it serves as a perfect introduction to the cultural wealth, the complexities and the dynamism of India which Jawaharlal Nehru likened to 'an ancient palimpsest on which layer upon layer of thought and reverie has been inscribed'. Delhi, too, is a may layered city, and is still changing.

Despite its being a burgeoning metropolis, Delhi offers surprising range of options to those who enjoy the outdoors. The river rain tract along the Yamuna, the dry scrubland forests of the Northern Ridge, natural and artificial lakes and the rockey outcrop near the Qutab complex allow for quiet as well as adventurous outdoor activities bird - watchers can enjoy a rich variety of bird life in Delhi, especially in the Ridge and the green areas surrounding the cities historic monuments.

In winter, the Delhi zoo is transformed into a small bird Sanctuary with migratory birds halting by its artificial lakes. Painted Strokes, Pintail Ducks, Bar headed Geese and spot bill Ducks are among the migratory birds which can be seen here. Delhi's tree - lined avenues are also reach in avian life. So are the forests of Ridge, which harbor more than 100 species of birds, from peacocks to predators. The Ridge is accessible through narrow paths that lead off Sardar

Patel Marg. Those in search of greater adventure can sample the thrills of aqua sports.

A multi-sports and leisure complex with all facilities for water sports- padal - boating, kayaking - canoeing and speed boating - has been created by Delhi Tourism at Bhaleswa Lake, situated on Delhi north - eastern edge. Fishing is also permitted here.

Delhi Tourism has also provided paddleboats at other water bodies in the heart of the city. These include the lakes near India Gate, Purana Qila- Prasad Nagar Lake and Naini Lake in Model Town. A variety of fiberglass boats have been acquired by the Corporation and can be hired at reasonable rates. Special training programs in kayaking and canoeing are organized at the latter too.

Delhi Tourism's Adventure Park at Lado Sarai extends a daring invitation to aspiring rock climbers. The wilderness here is ideal for adventures sports, and rock climbing is a year- round sport. Delhi Tourism provides the requisite equipment and training to scale the rocks in the vicinity of the Qutab Minar. Extended walk are also a fascinating option here given the rich variety of plants, flowers birds and insects. This exploration is throughout the year except the monsoon. Parasailing is another adventurous option.

Delhi Tourism can arrange Parasailing for beginners even at Kanwar Sheikha near Sohna in Haryana about 60 kms from Delhi. No advanced training or special skills are required to learn this inexpensive sport, which can be enjoyed by any one weighing between 40 kg and 80 kg, and without any element of risk under the watchful supervision of trained staff. Parasailing is under an open parachute with the aid of a special rope hooked up to a jeep. As the jeep moves, the parachute opens and the parasail or ascends to a height of about 100 mtrs. (Since the parasailing are limited in number and the flying hours regulated, booking will have to be made in advance).

Delhi Tourism has made a further contribution to the promotion of adventure sports by establishing the Adventure Club. This open to all Indian nationals above the age of 10. The club provides special packages in all adventure sports - parasailing, trekking, mountaineering expeditions, rock climbing, water sports, including white water rafting in the Ganga at Shivpuri, and adventure camps including the Ganga Adventure Package. A Water Sports Club has also recently been established by Delhi Tourism.

5

DATA ANALYSIS

RESPONSE OF THE TOUR OPERATORS

1. DO YOU OPERATE ONLY AT THE DOMESTIC LEVEL OR ONLY AT THE INTERNATIONAL LEVEL OR IN BOTH THE SECTORS?

- ❖ Only at the domestic level 33 per cent
- ❖ Only at the international level 15 per cent
- ❖ Both at the domestic and at the international level 62 per cent

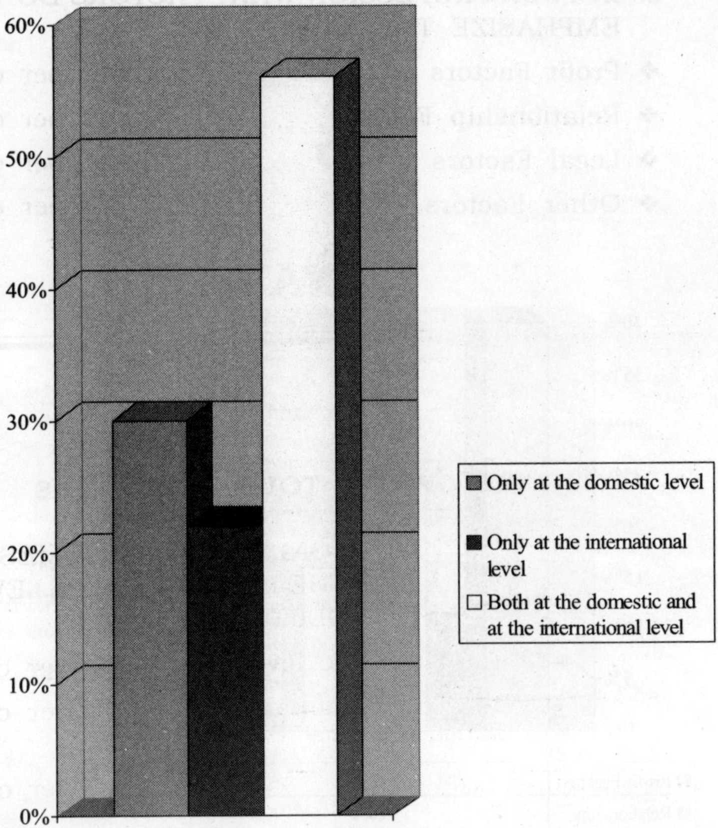

Only at the domestic level	30%
Only at the international level	22%
Both at the domestic and at the international level	56%

2. IN YOUR PROFESSION WHAT FACTORS DO YOU EMPHASIZE THE MOST?

- ❖ Profit Factors 40 per cent
- ❖ Relationship Factors 10 per cent
- ❖ Legal Factors 24 per cent
- ❖ Other Factors 16 per cent

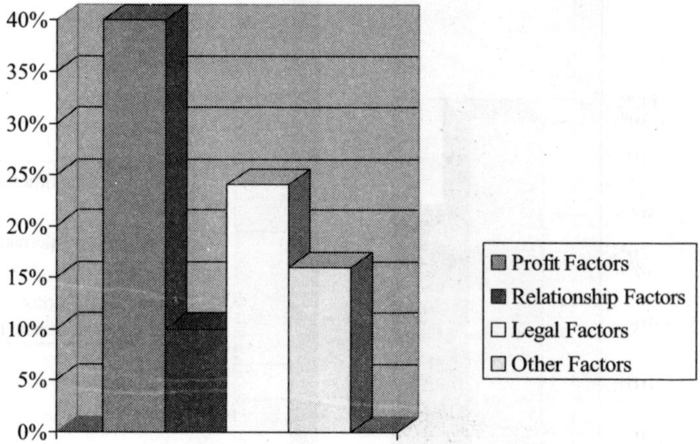

Profit Factors	40%
Relationship Factors	10%
Legal Factors	24%
Other Factors	16%

An analysis of the above response will suggest that most of the tour operators operating in the country are guided by profit motives.

3. DO YOU AGREE THAT CONSUMERS' INTEREST PROTECTION IS ONE OF YOUR PRIME RESPONSIBILITIES?

- ❖ Agree 80 per cent
- ❖ Disagree 10 per cent
- ❖ Do not know/Can not say 10 per cent

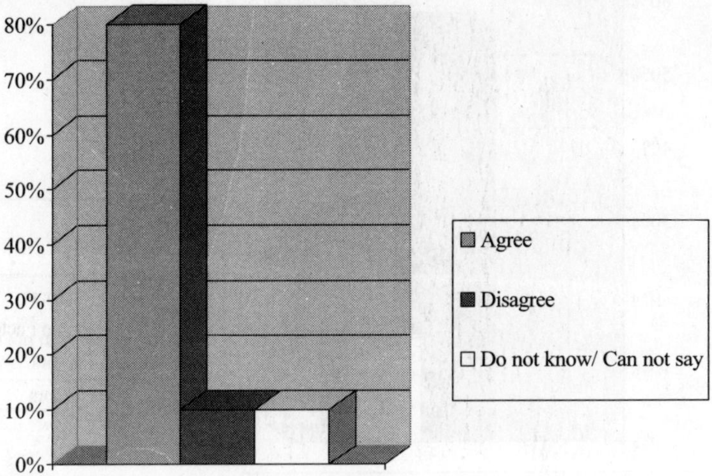

Agree	80%
Disagree	10%
Do not know/ Can not say	10%

80 per cent of the respondents agree to the proposition that consumers' interest protection is one of their prime responsibilities. However, agreeing to do something and putting the thing into action are two different points that need to be noted.

4. DO YOU AGREE THAT UNFAIR TRADE PRACTICES DO EXIST IN THE TRAVEL AND TOURISM INDUSTRY IN INDIA?

❖ Agree	32 per cent
❖ Disagree	54 per cent
❖ Do not know/Can not say	14 per cent

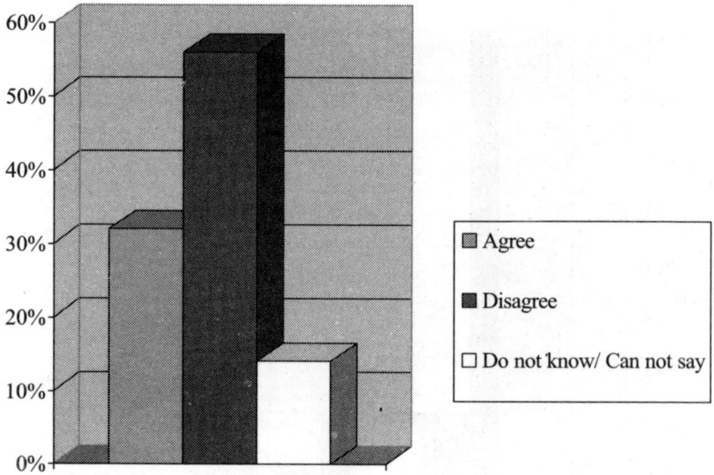

Agree	32%
Disagree	56%
Do not know/ Can not say	14%

The respondents in the travel and tourism industry who were studied gives an impression that unfair trade practices is not so rampant in the travel and tourism industry in India, given that 32 per cent of the respondents admitting the existence of these practices against 54 per cent who share a different thought.

5. ARE YOU AWARE ABOUT THE LEGAL ASPECTS OF CONSUMER PROTECTION IN THE TRAVEL AND TOURISM INDUSTRY?

- ❖ Yes 75 per cent
- ❖ No 15 per cent
- ❖ Do not know/ Can not say 15 per cent

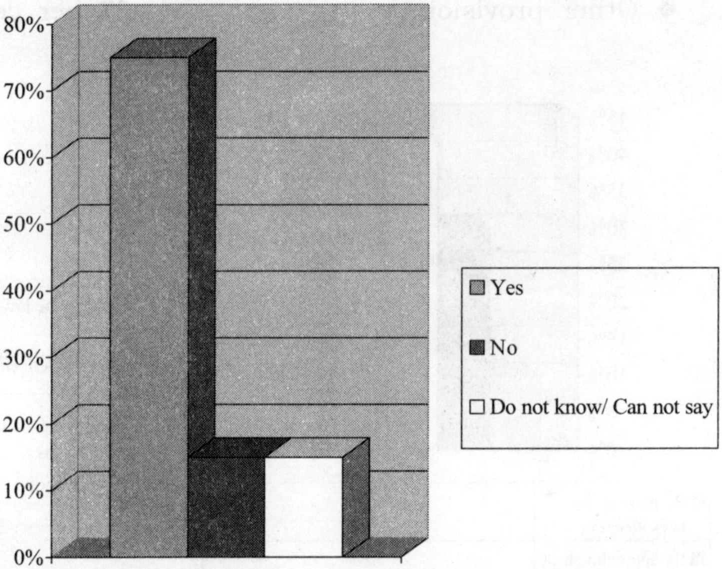

Yes	75%
No	15%
Do not know/ Can not say	15%

The travel and tour agents who constituted the sample of our study are aware about the legal aspects of the tourism and travel guidelines with respect to the consumer protection in the aforementioned industry.

6. HOW DO YOU THINK THE CONSUMERS' INTEREST CAN BE BETTER PROTECTED IN THIS INDUSTRY?

- ❖ By making the laws stricter 10 per cent
- ❖ By appointment of professionals 30 per cent
- ❖ BY practicing ethical tourism norms 42 per cent
- ❖ Other provisions 27 per cent

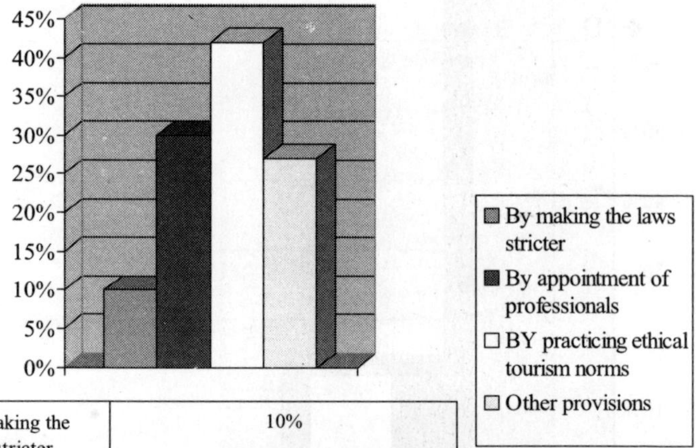

By making the laws stricter	10%
By appointment of professionals	30%
BY practicing ethical tourism norms	42%
Other provisions	27%

RESPONSE OF CONSUMERS IN THE INDUSTRY

7. WOULD YOU BE MORE LIKELY TO BOOK A HOLIDAY WITH A COMPANY IF THEY HAD A WRITTEN CODE TO GUARANTEE GOOD WORKING CONDITIONS, PROTECT THE ENVIRONMENT AND SUPPORT LOCAL CHARITIES IN THE TOURIST DESTINATION?

- Yes 52%
- No 33%
- Don't know 15%

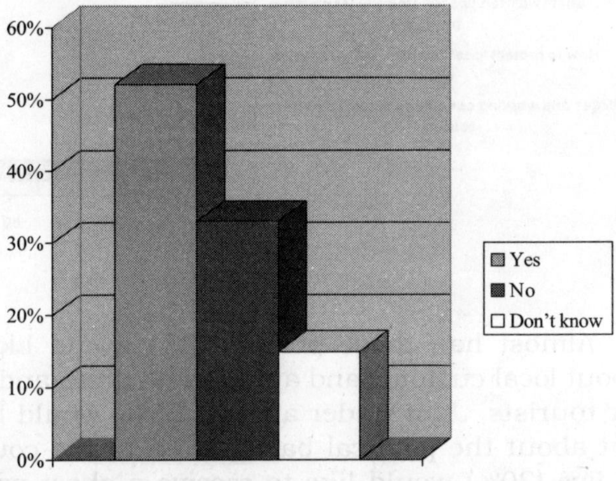

Yes	52%
No	33%
Don't know	15%

The evidence is clear. Holidaymakers are beginning to realise that their visits to exotic, sun-baked paradises have an impact on local people and environments. Increasingly, they want to ensure their holiday makes a positive contribution to local development. People appear willing to favour companies that can show they are bringing real benefits to those living in the destinations - and even to pay more for this peace of mind and better quality product.

8. IF YOU WERE GOING ON AN OVERSEAS HOLIDAY, WHAT TYPE OF INFORMATION WOULD YOU WANT TO HAVE CONCERNING YOUR HOLIDAY?

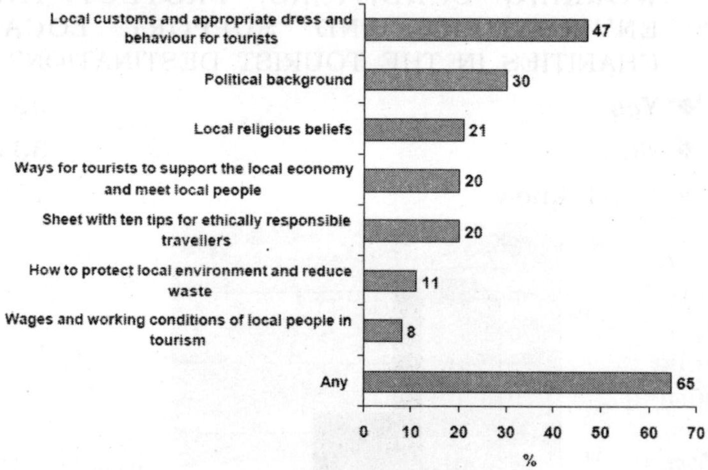

Almost half those polled (47%) would like to know about local customs and appropriate dress and behaviour for tourists. Just under a third (30%) would like to find out about the political background to the country. One in five (20%) would like to receive a sheet with 10 tips for ethically responsible travellers. The same number would also like to know ways that they can support the local economy and meet local people. Demand for information about the country visited is greater among younger than older people. Just over two-thirds of those aged from 15 to 54 (69%) would like to receive some information, compared with just over half (54%) of those aged 55+.

9. WHO DO YOU THINK HAS THE RESPONSIBILITY TO PROVIDE THIS INFORMATION?

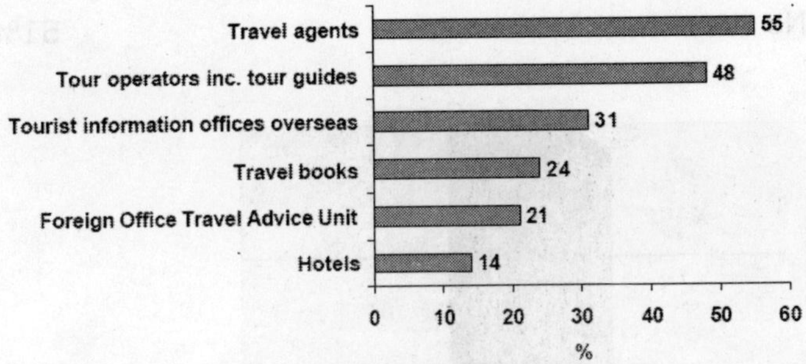

The tourism industry needs to take heed of public opinion and respond to consumer demand for more information. Since the same question was asked of the public two years ago, some operators have made more information available in their brochures, or on their websites, but the majority is still not providing the information that tourists want. This not only prevents tourists getting the most out of their holiday, but also prevents those in the destinations gaining from responsible tourist behaviour.

10. DO YOU THINK THAT WE HAVE A RESPONSIBLE TOURISM POLICY?

- ❖ Yes 49%
- ❖ No 51%

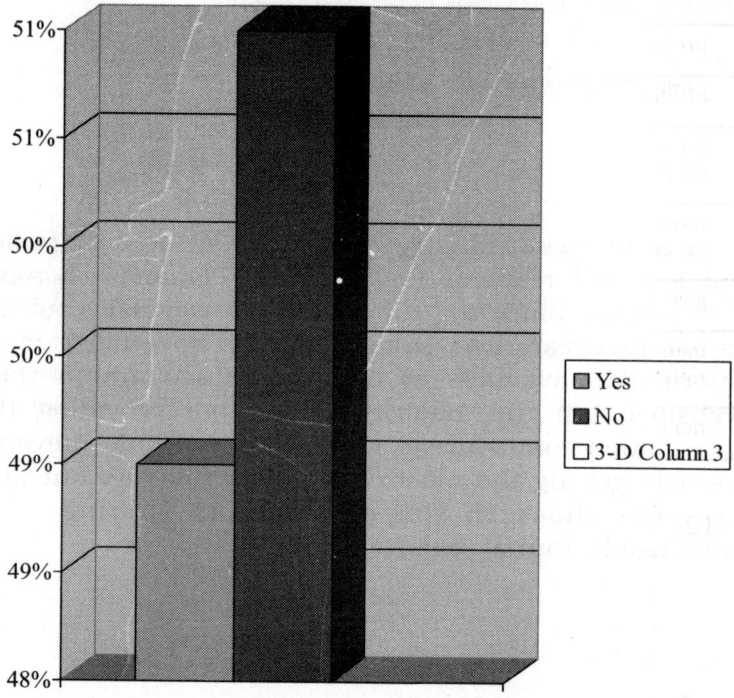

Yes	49%
No	51%
3-D Column 3	

The tourism industry has a long way to go to catch up with other industries, and much to do to satisfy consumer and investor pressure for responsible behaviour. CSR is here to stay and the pressure to adopt responsible business approaches will only increase.

11. WHICH OF THE FOLLOWING STATEMENTS WOULD YOU ASSOCIATE YOURSELF WITH? YOU MAY TICK AS MANY OR AS FEW AS YOU LIKE.

prefer just to switch off when I go on holiday	47%
have signed a petition in the last year	26%
prefer to travel independently	24%
attend church at least twice a month	15%
regularly buy fairly traded goods or use an ethical bank or investment fund	12%
have been on a trip to a developing country, or plan to do so in the next few years	12%
give more than 20 a month to charity	11%
member of an environmental, development or huaman rights group (such as RSPB or Amnesty International)	8%
none of these	18%

12. DO YOU AGREE THAT THE LEGAL SYSTEM IN INDIA IS ADEQUATE TO ENSURE EFFECTIVE CONSUMERS PROTECTION IN SUCH AN UNORGANIZED MARKET LIKE TRAVEL AND TOURISM?

- ❖ Agree 26 per cent
- ❖ Disagree 66 per cent
- ❖ Do not know/ Can not say 08 per cent

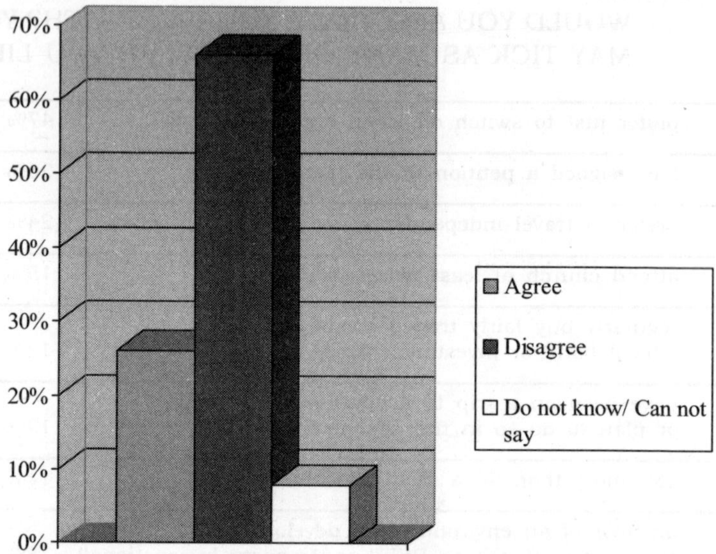

Agree	26%
Disagree	66%
Do not know/ Can not say	8%

13. DO YOU AGREE THAT WE NEED A SPECIAL MECHANISM LIKE THE CONSUMERS REDRESSAL FORUM FOR EFFECTIVE PROTECTION OF THE CONSUMER'S INTERESTS?

- ❖ Agree 57 per cent
- ❖ Disagree 12 per cent
- ❖ Do not know/ Can not say 31 per cent

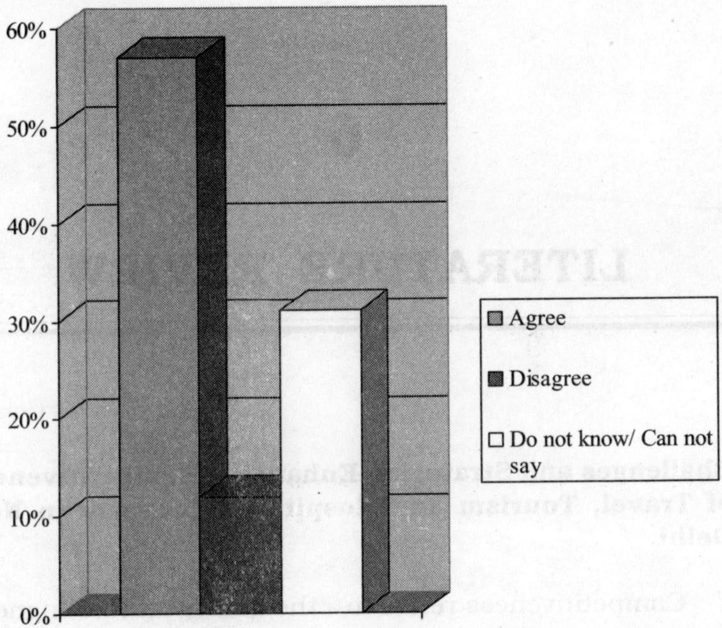

Agree	57%
Disagree	12%
Do not know/ Can not say	31%

6

LITERATURE REVIEW

Challenges and Strategies–Enhancing Competitiveness of Travel, Tourism and Hospitality Industry in New Delhi

Competitiveness refers to - the ability and willingness to compete and two most important underlying criteria of competitiveness are - 'Profitability' and 'Productivity', that is, increased competitiveness is reflected in sustained growth in productivity and profitability. Since 'productivity' and 'profitability' are vital for all organizations, industries, sectors and nations, it indicates that the concept of competitiveness is equally applicable to each of these entities, so it is a must that they appreciate the conceptual framework of competitiveness and the various forms that it takes, (commercial competitiveness, market competitiveness etc.) along with the fact that it is a complex ongoing process affected by a range of factors / inputs.

Although, 'competitiveness' in parlance of business (and industries) is not a new phenomenon and is usually discussed in terms of – the decisions it makes, the resources it has, and the environmental factors which surrounds the business, but lately, the trend of categorizing and evaluating nations on basis of their competitiveness has become a norm among economists, policy makers, business executives and investors. Liberalization, Privatization and Globalization (LPG) have worked together for reducing protection and creating a rapidly changing competitive environment resulting in fierce international competition 'in' and 'for' the world-market. With this, there has been a growing realization that avoiding the rigors of competition is not possible and developing strategies for enhancing sustainable competitiveness has emerged as a 'must do' exercise for all. However, the context of 'competitiveness' might vary for business, industries and nations, depending on their - objectives, form, nature and functions – that is - from completely social to hardcore commercial.

Competitiveness of Nations and the Service Sector - Most of the (developing) economies are in rapid transit towards becoming 'service economies" and therefore 'competitiveness of service sector' is emerging as a crucial factor influencing the overall competitiveness of a country, and India is no exception to this, where the share of services is increasingly getting higher in the total GDP1, and also the growth rate of India's 'service exports' is higher then the world average2, hence for India, out of the three pillars of competitiveness, one is certainly it's service sector (agriculture and manufacturing are the remaining two.)

Variables of Competitiveness at country, industry and firm level - The paper deals with the issue of competitiveness at all the three levels (country, industry and firm) taking - 'India' as the variable for 'country' and 'Indian Tourism and Hospitality Industry' as the variable for 'industry', and at the firm level, the paper identifies cases from many different organizations, rather then taking a particular organization as a variable, because a broader canvas is required to capture the diversity of businesses operating in this domain, and any one organization cannot symbolize the complete tourism and hospitality industry because this industry is formed by a combination of very different businesses. (Only infrastructure business, or only hotel business or only aviation business can not represent this industry alone, but all these businesses jointly do so).

The price competitiveness of travel and tourism: a comparison of 19 destinations- This paper presents findings and conclusions from an examination of the price competitiveness of 19 tourism destinations. Using Australia as a base country, the paper compares the prices of a bundle of tourist goods and services in a range of competing destinations, through the development of indices of international price competitiveness. Two major categories of prices are distinguished — those relating to travel to and from a destination (travel cost) and those relating to prices within the tourism destination (ground cost

Competitiveness Challenges of Tourism and Hospitality Industry – as mentioned above, different diverse businesses jointly form this industry (transportation, hotels, infrastructure, aviation etc), and a balanced development of all these different businesses and high coordination amongst all the participants is a prerequisite for enhancing competitiveness of this industry and creating this 'fine blend' of such 'polar elements' is a tough challenge in itself.

This industry can be called as the "industry of big paradoxes", first, on one hand it has almost unbeatable competitive advantages, huge potential and high growth rates3 (in terms of - generating foreign exchange, growth rates, & employment generation), and on the other hand, in spite of above mentioned positives, Indian Tourism and Hospitality Industry is still way behind even from its small neighbors in South-East Asia, not to mention the large counterparts like China.

Second paradox is that, on one hand, in order to be competitive, this industry needs the cooperation of both public and private sector players as both play a vital role in it, and on the other hand, cut throat competition also exists between the two in this industry itself. Finally, the 'offering' of this industry is also paradoxical. For India, where 'history' is an important attraction for tourists, this industry has to offer 'history', but it can not loose sight of modernization either, in other words, Indian Tourism and Hospitality Industry has to be a 'historian' and a 'futurist' simultaneously.

Thus, in order to find a sustainable solution to the competitiveness issue of this industry, the paper suggest that it is important to identify the reasons behind its lack of competitiveness and then to search for 'breakthrough solutions' to face the unique challenges it offers, by undertaking a study of the innovative and best practices developed and adopted by players of this industry in the global arena which are applicable in Indian conditions and finally, redefining the role of government and private players to create a more competitive landscape might also be an effective part of the overall solution.

Tourism in India has grown very much during the last decades. It gives the second highest net foreign exchange earnings to our economy. Foreign tourist arrivals are at 2.64 millions during 2000. Domestic tourism helps to understand various cultures and to experience national integration among the citizens. Apart from the higher class people, the middle class has emerged as a powerful source for the development of domestic tourism. Around 1.50 million domestic tourists have made a trip outside their places.

Environmental management of a tourist destination: A factor of tourism competitiveness

Although research to date has addressed various elements of destination competitiveness there has been little attempt to systematically and comprehensively study the environmental competitiveness from the managerial perspective. Since the Calgary tourism competitiveness model brought a systematic approach to tourism competitiveness research, this paper selectively uses its management element as a tool to link the competitiveness and environmental management. Following the model the destination management is divided into two parts: (1) managerial and (2) marketing efforts. This paper studies them from environmental perspective. First, destination environmental competitiveness can be increased by appropriate managerial efforts related to environmental impact (EI), and environmental quality (EQ) management. Second, the destination competitiveness can be enhanced through certain environmental marketing activities. Further, environmental management is categorized into groups: management by codes of conduct, by self-developed environmental practice, by certified or awarded best practice and by accreditation schemes. Their usefulness for environmental destination management and competitiveness is evaluated.

Determinants of Market Competitiveness in an Environmentally

Sustainable Tourism Industry

This article introduces a detailed new model of competitiveness that focuses on environmental sustainability factors associated with travel destinations. The multiplicity of industries involved in destinations' planning and development requires the use of a competitiveness model that examines the relationships among all stakeholders involved in creating and integrating value-added products to sustain resources while maintaining market position relative to other competitors. The development of future destinations must be guided by effective and efficient management with a focus on sustainable customer base. Thus, destination management should focus on a systematic examination of unique comparative advantages that provide a special long-term appeal to the target travel customer segments. Therefore, sustaining the longevity of a given destination becomes a function of responding to market demand and competitive challenges. It is critical for future destination development plans to be compatible with market needs and environment integrity for the industry to maintain its economic viability.

Tourism, Competitiveness, and Societal Prosperity

Each society is faced with the decision of how best to provide for the well-being and quality of life of its citizens. The choices involved span complex economic, socio-cultural, political, and environmental considerations. In particular, the economic base that a society chooses for itself has wide ranging ramifications. Increasingly, cities, states, and nations are turning to tourism as an important element in their economic portfolio as they recognize the potentially significant economic rewards at stake. Much of tourism development entails community development. If handled appropriately, tourism can become an important engine for achieving broader social goals. Whereas societies may aspire to achieve these goals, communities are struggling to manage tourism development effectively. Unfortunately, no integrative framework exists for managing all facets of tourism development. In this study the authors examine the link between societal prosperity and tourism using a competitiveness framework.

Strategic use of information technologies in the tourism industry

Information technologies (ITs) prevail in all functions of strategic and operational management. As information is the lifeblood of tourism, ITs provide both opportunities and challenges for the industry. Despite the uncertainty experienced in the development of ITs in tourism, the 'only constant will be change'. Increasingly, organizations and destinations, which need to compete will be forced to compute. Unless the current tourism industry improves its competitiveness, by utilizing the emerging ITs and innovative management methods, there is a danger for exogenous players to enter the marketplace, jeopardizing the position of the existing ones. Only creative and innovative suppliers will be able to survive the competition in the new millennium. This paper provides a framework for the utilization of technology in tourism by adopting a strategic perspective. A continuous business process re-engineering is proposed in order to ensure that a wide range of prerequisites such as vision, rational organization, commitment and training are in place, so they can enable destinations and principals to capitalize on the unprecedented opportunities emerging through ITs.

The Role of Awareness and Familiarity with a Destination: The Central Florida Case

This study is based on the theoretical background of the consumer's buying process incorporating product awareness, familiarity, interest, and purchase. Using a sample of 750 U.S. households, a series of hypotheses were tested to analyze whether consumer aware ness and familiarity with Central Florida as a vacation destination had an impact on the consumer's destination image and on the interest and likelihood to visit it. The results indicate that those who were familiar with Central Florida (i.e., had previously visited it) had a more positive image of the destination and were more interested in and likely to revisit it than those who were only aware of the destination. However, contrary to our expectations, interest or likelihood to visit Central Florida was not significantly higher among those who were aware of Central Florida as a tourist destination than those who were not aware of it. For this case, it is possible to conclude that as consumers move from the awareness stage to the familiarity stage their interest and likelihood to visit increase, although the same may not be true when consumers move from the no awareness to the awareness stage

TRAVEL INDUSTRY REGULATION

Business Practices and Consumer Protection Act

The Ministry of Public Safety and Solicitor General is responsible for consumer protection legislation, including the *Business Practices and Consumer Protection Act*. All travel agents and wholesalers located in British Columbia must be licensed under the Act and comply with the Travel Industry Regulation. This is the legislation under which travel agents and wholesalers are licensed and contribute to a Travel Assurance Fund, which compensates consumers who do not receive travel services they have purchased. However, the related Travel Industry Regulation requires updating.

The existing regulation does not address changes in the travel industry over the past three decades, or the related implications for consumers. For example, Internet sales and online reservations now allow travel agents and wholesalers to sell services to consumers worldwide. Travel agents can now conduct all or part of their business from their homes. And in British Columbia growing inbound tourism – particularly from Asia – is exposing the province's travel services and providers to international scrutiny.

To maximize fairness, equity and consumer protection in updating the Travel Industry Regulation, we are seeking input through written consultations.

Government plans two phases of consultation to inform its updating of the Travel Industry Regulation. As the first phase, this discussion paper focuses on the regulatory requirements for traditional travel agents and travel wholesalers, which sell such products as airline tickets, overseas tour packages and cruises.

A second discussion paper will address new sectors of the travel industry that have emerged and fall under the definition of "travel agent." Topics will include local tour operators, destination marketing organizations and strata ownership of vacation or hotel accommodations. The second discussion paper will be released in March 2008.

This consultation is an opportunity for you to provide feedback on how government can streamline regulatory requirements for travel agents and wholesalers while tightening gaps in consumer protection. Your comments are important and will help government to consider and develop proposals to update the Travel Industry Regulation

Source -Ministry of Public Safety and Solicitor General

Consultation on Travel Industry

Corporate Policy and Planning Office

Truth in Gaming: Toward Consumer Protection in the Gambling Industry

This article proposes a new regulatory regime, Truth in Gaming, designed to aid both recreational and problem gamblers alike, and based on the clear, accurate, and timely disclosure of the true costs of gambling. This proposal is based on research that indicates that pathological gamblers often engage in defective gambling strategies, misjudging their inability to control random events and evaluate their losses. The provision of accurate information about the true costs of gambling and the likelihood of losing may aid pathological and problem gamblers in their efforts to gain control over their gambling habits. Such information is crucial to providing consumer protection for gamblers, giving them the information they need to make informed decisions about whether, where, how often, and how much they gamble.

Unfortunately, gamblers are rarely provided with accurate price information for slot machines, and such information for other electronic gaming devices is often difficult for gamblers to determine. This lack of price information prevents gamblers from shopping effectively and so makes the market for gambling inefficient as casinos do not compete based on an obvious price for slot machines. Without this information, even non-problem gamblers may unwittingly take risks they would deem excessive if they knew the extent of those risks.

The article proposes a regulatory system, Truth in Gaming, that would require casinos to display accurate price information for slot machines and other gaming opportunities, in a way that is clear and meaningful, and that would be interactive so that it would reflect any changing costs based on, for example, how much money is bet. Each slot machine would display the hold percentage, the expected average loss percentage given the bet, for that machine and also a hold amount, which is the expected average amount lost given the bet. These are the true expected average cost of a bet, and should be disclosed to the gambler before the bet.

The article also proposes that gaming devices be configured so that gamblers can track their wins, losses, and hold percentages using smart cards, giving them the ability to accurately determine the true cost of gambling to them.

These proposals will force casinos to provide consumers the information that they need to bet rationally

Codes of ethics and tourism: An exploratory content analysis

The purpose of this paper was to investigate the content of a number of codes of ethics* from the tourism industry. To accomplish this objective, the researchers analyzed 414 statements from 40 codes of ethics based upon a theoretical framework. This framework was developed using ethical theory and locus of analysis (LOA) constructs. Six categories emerged from the data and were juxtaposed with the ethics-LOA theoretical framework. The results of this study demonstrate that codes of ethics are generally deontological in nature. Implications of this ethical orientation are discussed and recommendations for future code development are provided.

Ethical and responsible tourism: Consumer trends in the UK

Responsible tourism is emerging as a significant market trend in the UK as wider consumer market trends towards lifestyle marketing and ethical consumption spread to tourism. This paper reviews recent survey evidence about consumer attitudes towards the responsible and ethical aspects of the tourism they consume, and places this in the context of campaigns by Voluntary Service Overseas and Tear fund. Between 1999 and 2001 the percentage of UK holidaymakers aspiring to be willing to pay more for an ethical holiday increased by 7 per cent from 45 per cent to 52 per cent. The evidence for increasing consumer demand for responsible tourism is reported and the paper concludes with a discussion of the implications.

7

RECOMMENDATIONS FOR INDUSTRY AND TOURISTS

Industry

- Ensure that appropriate information is made available for tourists, especially on local customs and appropriate dress and behaviour and on ways to support the local economy and meet the local people when on holiday.
- Develop and implement ethical policies to enable tourism to be improved to support development from an economic, social and environmental perspective.
- Speak to people in developing country tourist destinations and to some of the development and environment groups who have partners on the ground. In this way the industry can gain a better understanding of some of the issues involved in tourism for the host communities and can listen to suggestions for ways to better support development.
- 'Rogue operators'—tourism operators who mistreat and take advantage of foreign tourists—have been

a longstanding issue for the tourism industry. It is an issue that unfortunately remains prevalent, as the committee heard throughout its inquiry. Serious concerns persist in the industry, particularly in major international destinations, about the activities of inbound and tour operators who do not operate to acceptable business and customer service standards. It seems that everyone agrees that rogue operators are a problem; however, there is far less agreement on what can be done to stop their operation. Essentially, there are two schools of thought on the solution. The first argues that there needs to be better enforcement of existing legislation in all jurisdictions, while the second contends that there needs to be new federal legislation introduced, which will require the licensing of all tour operators.

- There are a lot of anecdotes and rumour in relation to concerns, but upon working with the taskforce and meeting with the industry associations, we find as we drill down below the anecdotes to seek substantive information and facts there is very little evidence.

Tourists

As the public are booking their summer holiday overseas, especially to developing countries,

- Does the tour company provide adequate information on local customs, appropriate behaviour for tourists, ways to meet local people and support the local economy?
- Does the company have a written code of conduct which outlines its policies towards environmental protection, workers' rights and support for local development? Is a copy available?

- ❖ In what ways does the company try to ensure that its policies and practices support local development? Is there any literature to show this?

Independent travellers

A significant proportion of tourists do not go on package tours with the main tour operators. Many of these (24% according to the market research) describe themselves as independent travellers and they exercise more control over where they go, who they meet and what they spend their money on whilst on holiday. They have more freedom to make a positive impact and can do so in the following ways:

- ❖ Ask themselves some questions about their own holidays - how does my holiday support the local economy? In what ways can I learn about the context of the place I am visiting and behave in an appropriate manner when I am there?
- ❖ Visit tourism offices in their holiday destination to find out about local development projects or locally-run tourism developments. Support these initiatives.
- ❖ Explore the possibility of traveling with an tour operator that has more ethical policies and is supporting local development through their tours.

Tour Operators

The following 10 points cover the priority areas for action for tour operators:

- ❖ Establish a clear policy for responsible tourism and ensure that it covers operations both in the India and in overseas destinations, right through the supply chain. Ensure that any charitable giving is integrated into the business process and is focused on improving the situation in the destinations.

- ❖ Appoint a responsible tourism staff member who will oversee the development and integration of these issues throughout the organization. Ensure that there is also support for this at board level.
- ❖ Commit funds to becoming a more responsible operator in the areas of charitable giving, developing local business partnerships, training and giving advice to clients.
- ❖ Write down best practice and seek to learn from it, publicize it to clients and share it with others.
- ❖ Produce and disseminate a code for tourists to help them travel in a more informed and responsible way. Include advice on how they can support local charities.
- ❖ Take time to research destinations and speak to local development and environment groups and tourism associations, not just to the hotels. Find out which local businesses can be used, and with whom a partnership may be developed. This will enable the provision of better quality holidays.
- ❖ Work throughout the supply chain to develop and implement policies that will use local labour, local foods and local crafts. Make these policies available to suppliers.
- ❖ Build on health and safety guidelines for hotels to include social and environmental issues such as labour standards, minimum wage levels and good recycling and waste disposal systems.
- ❖ Set clear targets for year-on-year improvement in terms of building partnerships, using local suppliers and improving social and environmental conditions in hotels. Evaluate activities regularly, so that lessons can be learned.

- Use annual reports to publicize steps taken to promote responsible tourism, and to gain support among key stakeholders.

8

CONCLUSION

Tourism will expand greatly in future mainly due to the revolution that is taking place on both the demand and supply side. The changing population structure, improvement in living standard, more disposable income, fewer working hours and long leisure time, better educated people, ageing population and more curious youth in developing the countries, all will fuel the tourism industry growth. The arrival of a large number of customers, better educated and more sophisticated, will compel the tourist industry to launch new products and brands and re-invents traditional markets. The established traditional destinations founded on sun-sea-sand products will have to re-engineer their products. They must diversify and improve the criteria for destinations and qualities of their traditional offers. Alongside beach tourism, the tourism sector will register a steady development of new products based on natural rural business, leisure and art and culture. Thus the study of new markets and emerging markets and necessity of diversified products are the basis of our strategy, which can enhance and sustain, existing and capture new markets.

Marketing mix is a mixture of elements, which interact and complement each other to achieve the targeted results. It is the mixture of controllable marketing variables that the firm uses to pursue the sought level of sales in the target market. It is a combination of the amounts and marketing variables which any firm uses at a particular time in order to achieve results.

A tourist enterprise can use combination of specific activities to achieve the best results. A firm can decide which of them to use, how, when, and where to use and which resources to allocate to them.

Special forces bearing of the marketing mix in travel and tourism are consumers buying behaviour (their motives buying habits etc.), the travellers behaviour, their practices structure etc., Competitors position and behaviours, government its control of pricing and promotional practices.

In deciding on the marketing, program a company must decide to law much to adapt its marketing mix (product, price, promotion, place) to local condition. At the two ends of the spectrum are standardized and adopted marketing mix with many steps in between.

Marketing mix helps the marketing manager whether individual or firm or official tourism organization-NTO, RTO, to understand where marketing action, can be initiated to improve the acceptability of a tourist product and stimulate the demand. It help in understand clearly what marketing is all about, helps in integrated approach to marketing, and in avoiding losing sight of the market forces related to the efforts.

Where the responsible tourism elements make for a superior product it will attract consumers predisposed to purchase. The responsible tourism product has one particular advantage over many other ethical products — the consumer will often experience the difference. A cup of fairly traded coffee or tea will not taste significantly different from other teas and coffees — it can taste as good but not better. Responsible tourism holidays which bring particularly high-quality engagement with local communities and their environments can provide a superior product, the life-enhancing experience which a growing sector of the market craves.

Present five year plan gives importance to:

- ❖ Development of infrastructure
- ❖ Development of trekking, winter sports, wildlife and beach resorts
- ❖ Exploring new source markets in region and countries having cultural affinity
- ❖ Environmental protection and cultural preservation of national heritage projects
- ❖ Launching of national image buildings and marketing plans
- ❖ Providing inexpensive accommodation in different tourist centers
- ❖ Streaming of facilitation procedures at airports
- ❖ Human resource development
- ❖ Creating awareness
- ❖ Facilitating private sector participation in development of infrastructure

DEVELOPMENT AND CHALLENGES IN THIS INDUSTRY

Organizations

Department of Tourism (Under the Minister of Civil Aviation & tourism)

It formulates and implements the polices and program for tourism development. It attracts foreign tourist by developing infrastructure, publicity and promotion, travel agencies, etc. It as 21 filed officers in India providing facilitation services. 18 officers are functions in overseas countries to attract tourist to India with Air India it makes joint promotional effects in US, UK, Europe, Australia and other countries.

India tourism development corporation (ITDC)

It is a public sector units established in 1966. It is involved in construction, management and marketing of hotels restaurants, etc. Tourist transport facilities, production, distribution and seal of tourist published materials, providing entertainment facilities, etc. are some of the services rendered by ITDC

Indian institution of Tourism and Travel management

It is an autonomous body to educate tourism and travel management for tourism personnel. It also organizes entrepreneurship development programs, seminar, workshops, etc.

Institutes of Hotel Management & Catering Technology

It offers various degree/diploma courses relating to Hotel Management, nutrition, etc at various parts of the country.

National Institute of water sports

It is set up in Goa and conducts courses like sailing, scuba diving, water skiing, etc.

Need for attention

The average global growth of the industry is 5% but the tourist traffic share of India is static at 0.38%.

Neighboring countries have utilized the opportunity for their growth. Due to the effect of 26/11 attack, September 11 attack in Asia-pacific region, there was a loss of 4.4 million jobs. Also, there was 5.7% loss in tourism demands.

Awaiting opportunities in this sector

India is distinct in having

- Ancient Civilization
- Natural landscape
- Traditions
- Music, dance
- Religious practices
- Exclusive festivals
- Art & Craft

Focus of the international traveler is shifting from developed regions to the developing regions.

Challenges to be faced

- Many of the tourist site environments are unhealthy
- Facilities and services are poor in many sites
- There exists inadequate transportation to reach and continue the journey
- Infrastructure facility is very poor
- There is limited availability of tourism information at limited places
- There are regional conflicts due to which tourism is getting affected in some areas
- There is a lack of adequate security in some areas of the country which makes the tourists feel insecure

Overcoming challenges

- ITDC have to be enriched so that it can provide adequate facilities at tourist sites like good environment, tourism information, etc.
- Present modes of transports are getting strengthened. However, the reaching tourist spots from the nearby town/city is still a difficult one. Special attention has to be paid by the Department of tourism so that its recommendation has to be implemented by the Government at the earliest.
- The Central and state Governments, must have special attention and invest in large to develop the infrastructure for utilizing the tourist spots.
- Tourism information must be updated often. The websites must give enriched information's with catchy phrases. Specific toll free numbers can be used for easy access of information by tourists
- The Government must take action to solve security problems and regional conflicts.
- Liberalizing the visa norms can be made so that more number of tourists can arrive and stay for more days.
- Involvement of private sector in the field can be made to serve the tourists better
- Investment in HRD programmes relating to travel & tourism industry can help to promote it better
- There can be focused promotion of various places to get attention of the travellers by using aids like short films, photographs, etc.
- Clearly planned, focused tour packages can be introduced which may attract the travellers

It is clear that there is a wide scope for underdeveloped countries like India to promote tourism.

If India overcomes the challenges by enriching its present strategies, it will emerge as a best tourist spot and will yield maximum foreign exchange to our country. 'Shining India's' economic buoyancy has shown a significant growth of 16.5% in tourist arrivals in year 2003 with a record growth in foreign exchange earnings of 20%. Industry sources reveal that India's annual real growth of the travel & tourism sector is poised to increase by 8.8 % between 2004-2014, higher than China, Laos, Vietnam and Fiji. It is estimated that the 8.8% growth will create a yawning gap in demand & supply, thus creating an enormous need for professionals in the travel and tourism industry. Globally tourism will account for 11,404,000 jobs of total employment which in turn will create both directly and indirectly in 2004, 24,456,600 jobs in India. Further, by 2014 there would be 27,790,000 tourism jobs in India. With this rapid increase in travel & tourism jobs India will be the second largest travel & tourism employer in South Asia. Thus, the future is deep vested in tourism... the key to being a part of this fast growing industry is harness the best skills for being a professional in the travel & tourism industry.

The Indian market is growing rapidly in all three industry sectors of Airlines, Logistics and Travel. Kale plans to increase its focus on the domestic market and bring its global experience and world-class platforms to the Indian industry. The growth in the logistics industry is directly related to the growth in the Indian economy. With India's gross domestic profit (GDP) growing at over 9 per cent per year and the manufacturing sector enjoying double digit growth rates, the Indian logistics industry is expected to reach a market size of over $125 billion by 2010.The corporate travel industry in India is highly unorganized, like the leisure travel industry, with many small and medium size players servicing very few corporate or SMEs. This presents a huge opportunity for travel companies to harness technology and improve processes and offerings. A rough estimate would put the corporate travel industry worth close to Rs. 10,000 crore and a growth rate of 30% Y.Y. India is also becoming a power market for online travel management. Phocus Wright Inc. says the online travel industry in India is expected to grow to Rs. 8,500 crore by 2008.

Initiative by Delhi Tourism Development Corporation DTTDC

Delhi Tourism Development Corporation, an undertaking of the Government of Delhi, was incorporated in December 1975 to promote tourism in Delhi.

Initiative taken by the government

Dissemination of Tourism Related information

To give reliable information on historical and cultural facets of the city and various tourist related services being imparted by the corporation, tourist information and assistance counters have been strategically located at major points of disembarkation in the city.

Tourist Services

The Corporation offers value based city sight seeing tours and innovative package tours to Places of historic, cultural and scenic interest and to places of pilgrimage. Leave Travel Concession Tours are arranged for the Government servants. Detailed tour information is provided from information offices of the Corporation and through advertisement in the print media.

Adventure Activities

Delhi Tourism's infrastructure network and trained outdoor staff helps to choose from the various options available for satisfying penchant for adventure. Trekking in the high mountains, rock climbing, parasailing and water sports activities are offered.

Dilli Haat

In its endeavor to develop tourism related infrastructure Dilli Haat is being operated by DTTDC, a Permanent food and craft bazaar. It was developed in collaboration with NDMC and the Ministry of Textiles, Government of India it was primarily planned to provide a venue to craft persons to sell their wares directly to the regional cuisines of the country.

Musical Fountain

Delhi Tourism 's Musical fountain at Ajmal Khan Park is spread over an area of five acres. Water cascades to the synchronized music and coloured lights in a 20 minutes shop.

Manpower training for the tourism industry

Delhi Chapter of the Indian Institute of Tourism and Travel Management (IITM) under the administrative control of the corporation conducts training programmes for the tourism industry. Regular programmes are announced through advertisements in print media and details are available from the Institute

Hotel Industry

Delhi's hotel industry is also seeing fresh investment Delhi has 70 star hotels, which include 24 5-star deluxe and 5-star hotels. Eden Park Hotels is investing US$ 22 million in the renovation of Qutab hotel. The state government plans to further develop tourism through information centers, pilgrimage tour packages and tourist sports complexes.

Restoration of Denotified Monuments

Delhi is a city of monuments and government has taken steps to preserve the rich cultural heritage of the city and to restore various denotified monuments

Sources :www.indianbusiness.nic.in

The future research on these topics are:

- Suitable Plans for the Upcoming Commonwealth Games reference to consumer protections.
- Government Policy and Measures Adopted for the International Tourists.
- Special aspects For the Development of Travel and Tour Operators.
- Training and development by the government for the tours operator and travel agencies for the upcoming Commonwealth Games.

The future research will be centered on the facilities provided for the influx of comparatively higher number of Foreign Tourists than the normal inflow of International travelers. Consumer protection should be an essential focus area for our government and more policy decisions and laws should be made to protect International and Domestic Tourists alike, which will be an essential area of my study.

PhoCus Wright Inc. says the online travel industry in India is expected to grow to Rs.8500 crore by 2008-09.

REFERENCES

1. Fennel A David, Ecotourism: An introduction. Routledge, London and New York, 1999.
2. Page J Stephen, Brunt Paul, Bushy Graham and Connel Jo, Tourism: A modern Synthesis. . Thompson Learning.2001
3. Gour Kanchilal, Indian Tourism through Inner eyes, Prabhat Agency, 2005
4. 1982. Turnout for Games Lags, New Delhi Paper Says. *The New York Times*. November 26.
5. Afsal, M. 2005. Over six lakh hawkers may face evacuation before the games. The Age, June 07.
6. Andreff, W *Sport in developing countries*
7. http://www.sportanddev.org/data/document/document/143.pdf
8. . Baade, R and Matheson, V. 2002. Bidding for the Olympics: Fool's Gold? *Transatlantic Sport: The Comparative Economics of North American and European Sports, (London: Edward Elgar Publishing, 2002), 127-151.*
9. — 2003. *Mega-Sporting Events in Developing Nations: Playing the Way to Prosperity?* http://www.williams.edu/Economics/wp/mathesonprosperity.pdf
10. Baviskar, A. 2005. A lifeline ... under siege. *The Hindu,* November 06.

11. Boralkar, D. B.; Mukharjee, U.; Singh, S. B. 1986. Increase of lead concentration in ambient air during the IX Asian games, New Delhi, 1982 as indicated by the plants. *Indian Journal of Air Pollution Control 1986; 7(2): 65-7.*

12. Brevik, Tore J. 30.July 2005, *The Role of Sporting Events in Developing Countries.* Presentation at the Global Sports Alliance SPORTS SUMMIT FOR THE ENVIRONMENT (SSE) 2005. 30.July 2005, Nagoya Norakudo

13. Brown, A and Massey, J. 2001. *Literature Review: The Impact of Major Sporting Events.* http://www.uksport.gov.uk/images/uploaded/M2002_Baseline_2001.pdf

14. Brunet, F. 1995. *An economic analysis of the Barcelona'92 Olympic Games: resources, financing and impact* [online article]. Barcelona: Centre d'Estudis Olímpics UAB. [Consulted: 26/05/06] <http://olympicstudies.uab.es/pdf/wp030_eng.pdf>

15. Cambridge Policy Consultants. (2002). *The Impact of the Manchester 2002 Commonwealth Games. Manchester: Manchester City Council* http://www.sportdevelopment.org.uk/manimpactcpc.pdf (accessed-29-05-06)

16. Chatterjee, M.B. 2006. JBIC completes project appraisal for funding Delhi metro Phase II *The Business Line,* Jan 28

17. Delhi to get 25 more flyovers. 2006. *The Hindu,* Jan 04.

18. DDA 'go-ahead' to many projects. 2006. *The Hindu,* May 06.

19. Draft Master Plan for Delhi-2021. 2005. Delhi Development Authority. Delhi.

20. Aronsson Lars, the Development of Sustainable Tourism. Continuum London & New York 20005. Mohan Puri, Gianchand, Tourism management, Pragun Publications, New Delhi 2006.

21. Blangy, Sylvie and Megan Epler Wood (1992). "Developing and implementing ecotourism guidelines for wildlands and neighbouring communities." In "Ecotourism: A Guide for Planners and Managers." Edited by Kreg Lindberg and Donald E. Hawkins. Ecotourism Society Publication.

22. IUCN (1996). "Tourism, ecotourism and protected areas." SADAG, France.

23. G.A.P Adventure (www.gapadventures.com/sustainable_tourism/responsible_traveller)

24. Tearfund (2000) 'Tourism an Ethical Issue, Market Research Report', Tearfund, London.

25. *Ibid.* — 42 per cent said that it would make no difference; 13 per cent said no.

26. Tearfund (2002) 'Worlds Apart', Tearfund, London.

27. A sample of 963 respondents surveyed face to face by MORI in the street in the period 2nd–24th September, 2000, in 107 constituency- based sampling points; data weighted to reflect the profile of British holidaymakers. In 2002 the same methodology was used with 713 respondents; the fieldwork dates were 10th–25th September, 2002.

28. Tearfund (2001) 'Tourism Putting Ethics into Practice', Tearfund, London.

29. United Nations Environment Programme at website: www.unep.org

30. Tourism Market Trends: 2001 edition. World Overview and Tourism Topics. World Tourism Organisation and website: www.world-tourism.org

31. Pro-Poor Tourism Strategies: Making tourism work for the poor. Ashley, Roe, Goodwin, 2001.

32. Holiday Purchasing Patterns Market Assessment, Key Note, 2001.

33. Tourism Concern at the website: www.tourismconcern.org.uk

34. Travel Trends: A Report on the 2000 International Passenger Survey. National Statistics, 2001.

35. Roy, S. 2006. See you in Delhi....No, not yet. *The Indian Express*, April 02.

36. Information website: www.infoplease.lycos.com

37. Tearfund guide to tourism: Don't forget your ethics, Tearfund, June 2000.

APPENDIX

QUESTIONNAIRE

1. DO YOU OPERATE ONLY AT THE DOMESTIC LEVEL OR ONLY AT THE INTERNATIONAL LEVEL OR IN BOTH THE SECTORS?

- ❖ Only at the domestic level — 33 per cent
- ❖ Only at the international level — 15 per cent
- ❖ Both at the domestic and at the international level — 62 per cent

2. IN YOUR PROFESSION WHAT FACTORS DO YOU EMPHASIZE THE MOST?

- ❖ Profit Factors — 40per cent
- ❖ Relationship Factors — 10 per cent
- ❖ Legal Factors — 30 per cent
- ❖ Other Factors — 20 per cent

3. DO YOU AGREE THAT CONSUMERS' INTEREST PROTECTION IS ONE OF YOUR PRIME RESPONSIBILITIES?

- ❖ Agree — 76 per cent
- ❖ Disagree — 20 per cent
- ❖ Do not know/ Can not say — 04 per cent

4. DO YOU AGREE THAT UNFAIR TRADE PRACTICES DO EXIST IN THE TRAVEL AND TOURISM INDUSTRY IN INDIA?

- ❖ Agree 30 per cent
- ❖ Disagree 56 per cent
- ❖ Do not know/ Can not say 14 per cent

5. ARE YOU AWARE ABOUT THE LEGAL ASPECTS OF CONSUMER PROTECTION IN THE TRAVEL AND TOURISM INDUSTRY?

- ❖ Yes 70per cent
- ❖ No 15 per cent
- ❖ Do not know/ Can not say 15 per cent

6. HOW DO YOU THINK THE CONSUMERS' INTEREST CAN BE BETTER PROTECTED IN THIS INDUSTRY?

- ❖ By making the laws stricter 10 per cent
- ❖ By appointment of professionals 30 per cent
- ❖ BY practicing ethical tourism norms42 per cent
- ❖ Other provisions 27 per cent

7. WOULD YOU BE MORE LIKELY TO BOOK A HOLIDAY WITH A COMPANY IF THEY HAD A WRITTEN CODE TO GUARANTEE GOOD WORKING CONDITIONS, PROTECT THE ENVIRONMENT AND SUPPORT LOCAL CHARITIES IN THE TOURIST DESTINATION?

- ❖ Yes 52%
- ❖ No 33%
- ❖ Don't know 15%

8. IF YOU WERE GOING ON AN OVERSEAS HOLIDAY, WHAT TYPE OF INFORMATION WOULD YOU WANT TO HAVE CONCERNING YOUR HOLIDAY?

9. WHO DO YOU THINK HAS THE RESPONSIBILITY TO PROVIDE THIS INFORMATION?

10. DO YOU THINK THAT WE HAVE A RESPONSIBLE TOURISM POLICY?

- Yes 49%
- No 51%

11. WHICH OF THE FOLLOWING STATEMENTS WOULD YOU ASSOCIATE YOURSELF WITH? YOU MAY TICK AS MANY OR AS FEW AS YOU LIKE.

12. DO YOU AGREE THAT THE LEGAL SYSTEM IN INDIA IS ADEQUATE TO ENSURE EFFECTIVE CONSUMERS PROTECTION IN SUCH AN UNORGANIZED MARKET LIKE TRAVEL AND TOURISM?

- Agree 26 per cent
- Disagree 66 per cent
- Do not know/ Can not say 08 per cent

13. DO YOU AGREE THAT WE NEED A SPECIAL MECHANISM LIKE THE CONSUMERS REDRESSAL FORUM FOR EFFECTIVE PROTECTION OF THE CONSUMER'S INTERESTS?

- Agree 57 per cent
- Disagree 12 per cent
- Do not know/ Can not say 31 per cent